Life After Suicide

The Survivor's Grief Experience:

Revised Edition

Terence W. Barrett PhD

Praise For *Life After Suicide: The Survivor's Grief Experience,* by Terence W. Barrett, PhD

"I have read many books about suicide and grief, looking for "just the right one" to help my brother through his ordeal. I got lucky one day and found this wonderful book. He said it has helped him more than anyone or anything."

A Survivor
Little Rock, Arkansas

"I do not have the words to describe how much this book has helped me. Our Chaplain gave me a copy. Lots of my husband's comrades tried to find comforting words to write or say when they came home. I send them quotes from this book and suggest that they read *Life After Suicide* for themselves. Reading it has been better for me than anything anyone has said or done since the suicide."

A Veteran's wife
New York, New York

"I was fortunate to find this book at the library. I found answers to questions I wouldn't have even thought to ask. The information is written in such a way that I got the help I needed without even knowing that I needed it."

A Survivor
San Clemente, California

"My colleagues in ministry recommended this book as the <u>most</u> helpful resource for those who must survive the suicide of a loved one."

A Pastor
Gahanna, Ohio

"I did not completely understand the experience of the parents and husbands and wives on the Reserve and had no idea how to provide a compassionate response to them following the suicides. After reading this book, my path seemed clearer to me. Before a new member attends our group, I now give them a copy of *Life After Suicide*, ask them to read it cover to cover, and welcome them to bring their questions and tears to the next meeting."

A Nurse
Winnipeg, Manitoba, Canada

Life

After

Suicide

Also by Terence W. Barrett, PhD:

The Search for the Forgotten Thirty-Four: Honored by the U.S. Marines, Unheralded in Their Hometowns?

Remembering James Edmund Johnson, USMC: Pocatello's "Number One Hero of the Korean War"

Remembering Douglas Eugene Dickey, USMC: "Reaching the Finest and Most Noble Heights"

TERENCE W. BARRETT, PhD

Life After Suicide:

The Survivor's Grief Experience

Published by Aftermath Research, P.O. Box 5551, Fargo, ND, 58102.

Books can be ordered individually or in bulk at the address above.

Copyright © 2013, 1989 by Terence W. Barrett PhD

All rights reserved, with the exception of brief passages for the purposes of review or research.

First Edition / November 1989
Revised Edition / November 2013

Library of Congress Cataloging-in-Publication Data
Barrett, Terence W., 1949-

Includes bibliographical references.
ISBN-10: 149287454X
ISBN-13: 9781492874546

Lyrics to *Letter to a Suicide Survivor,* Copyright © January 15, 1993, by Rachel Barrett, are reprinted with permission.

Lyrics to *Not Forgiven,* Copyright © 2007, by Brenda Weiler, are reprinted with permission.

1. Suicide Grief. 2. Bereavement 3. Survivors. 4. Psychology. 5. Mental Health.

Printed in the United States of America

Letter to a Suicide Survivor

Dear Loved One,

If I could there are many things,
I would have you know about me.
I didn't tell you much when I was alive,
Not because you wouldn't listen,
But because I could not tell you,
There is no way you could have known why I died.

Now if I could only tell you,
If I could only reach you,
If you could only hear me say,
I love you so, I love you so.

I was hurting, I was mostly afraid.
I was hiding, I tried to be brave,
But the darkness shut out the light.
I was falling, and you reached out your hand,
I was crying with my secret plan,
And you answered, but I could not respond.

And loved one,
I'm sorry my decision has brought you such pain.
I gave you no time for goodbyes.
I could never see the beauty of love around me,
The beauty in you, especially in you.

You are blameless, there was nothing to say.
I just wanted release from my pain.
I am free now, and I walk in the light.
I'll be with you, as the days glimmer by,
Let it go now, let it float to the sky,
And remember, I know how you tried.

And now I can tell you,
And now I can reach you,
Now you can hear me say,
I love you so,
You loved me so.

Rachel Barrett
1993

Contents

Acknowledgments	xvii
FOREWORD	xix
PREFACE	xxi
ONE. Suicide: A Way of Dying	1
TWO. The Grieving Survivor	17
THREE. The Grief Complex	25
FOUR. The Tidal Wave After Suicide	37
FIVE. It's the Same, But Different	49
Initial Grief Reactions	
SHOCK	50
DISBELIEF	51
SEVERE SORROW	52
Primary Grief Reactions	56
PREOCCUPATION WITH THE DECEASED	58
GUILT	60
ANGER	64
DEPRESSION	66
LONELINESS	71
FLIGHT INTO ACTIVITY	73

NEED TO TALK	75
FEELING DESERTED	76
RELIEF	78
Later Grief Reactions	79
LOSS OF SELF-WORTH	80
SELF-DESTRUCTIVE BEHAVIOR	84
PHYSICAL ILLNESS	87
WITHDRAWAL OR ISOLATION	90
IDEALIZATION	92
LOSS OF LIBIDO	95
SIX. Because Suicide Can Be So Unexpected	99
SEARCH FOR EXPLANATION	100
TAKING RESPONSIBILITY	109
FEELING BLAMED	113
VIVID MEMORIES OF THE DEATH	114
DYSFUNCTIONAL RELATIONSHIPS	117
SEVEN. It Didn't Have To Be This Way	125
PREVENTABLE DEATH	126
STIGMA	128
DELIBERATE ABANDONMENT	133
EIGHT. No Other Survivor Could Imagine	135
DENIAL OF THE CAUSE OF DEATH	136
REJECTION	140
EMBARRASSMENT	142
FEAR OF INSANITY	143
THE DEATH AS A MORAL ISSUE	145
COMMUNICATION PROBLEMS	147
NINE. The Aftermath	151
TEN. Surviving Suicide Bereavement	169

ELEVEN. Further Conclusions	185
NOTES	197
SELECTED RESOURCES	207
ABOUT THE AUTHOR	209

Acknowledgments

I wish to thank those who provided help, support, and encouragement in the completion of this revised edition of the original book.

My heartfelt thank you goes to my wife, Rachel Dittmer Barrett, for her meticulous proofreading of the manuscript and for her thoughtful and creative suggestions. She has been a part of this endeavor from the beginning.

My thanks to Dr. Thomas Scott for his guidance during the initial stages of this research and to Sister Jane Walker and Lana Palmberg for their early efforts to establish a suicide survivors support group in Fargo in the mid-1980s. Their encouragement and assistance in contacting suicide survivors was an important part in the gathering of survivors' statements for this book.

My gratitude and respect go to all the survivors who have warmly welcomed me into their lives and trustingly shared their grief experiences with me over the span of nearly thirty years. Although each of their experiences was personal and unique in its own ways, the similarities within their encounters with grief are the subject of this book.

I am grateful for having had the privilege to serve on the American Foundation for Suicide Prevention North Dakota Chapter Board of Directors for six years with many dedicated men and women. Their efforts to provide support to suicide survivors and to enlist community involvement in suicide prevention initiatives are truly inspiring. Their "Get it done" attitudes continue to make a difference.

I appreciate the interest expressed by Paul and Patty Becka, Eric and Pati Walz, Ron and Kitty Maltarich, Mike Kolody, Daniel and Cheri Reed, Dennis and Maureen Salettel, Tom and Susan Boardman, and Don and Pam Sandborg across thirty years. Their friendship remains a constant in my life. Longtime friends who gather together annually have also expressed their enthusiasm for this work and were among the first to read these pages: Joe Arnold, James Barry, Kevin Byrne, Richard Clark, Tim Cleary, Tom Coughlin, Gerald Fallon, Michael Feighan, Tim Harkness, Kevin Keegan, Regis McGann, Tim McManamon, Kevin O'Malley, and John Richilano.

Special thanks to Carl Wichman for his suggestions in the completion of the first edition of this book and to Scott Minot for his skilled technical help in restructuring this revised edition from the first publication.

I extend my appreciation to Timothy Teig, David Seifert, Denise Leeby, Lavon Schmidt, and Christy Wagner Karst of the Fargo VET Center for their efforts on behalf of our combat veterans and their families.

Terence W. Barrett
Fargo, North Dakota
2013

Foreword

There are very few books that provide this level of insight about the struggles and despair that consumes a person after the death of a loved one by suicide. After the loss of my daughter, Jen, to suicide in 2005, I was lost in a vast consuming darkness. I felt the world to be a cold and lonely place. I felt removed from life, and the value of my existence became diminished within me. I experienced shame, abandonment, deep sorrow and overwhelming guilt. My road to recovery was not easy, but few worthwhile things in our lives are easy.

This book is a forthright effort to revitalize the discussion on how survivors of suicide loss cope and adjust to the traumatic death of their loved one. That suicide touches the very core of our humanness is the central theme of this book. It helps us understand that suicide bereavement is more than common grief. It helps us understand the special grief reactions that are most common to survivors of suicide loss. These reactions include searching for a reason, taking responsibility for the death, questioning why, and dealing with anger and guilt.

Although this book helps us understand the differences in the initial, primary and later grief reactions, the description of stigma, the invisible wound that burns a survivor emotionally, psychologically and mentally is what sets this book apart from others. Life After Suicide clearly describes that the challenge for all survivors is to know that society tends to view suicide as abnormal. The book asks the relevant questions: Can we stop viewing suicide as a sin? Can we stop saying it is a weakness of character or an act of insanity or selfishness?

The beliefs and insensitive words of our culture deprive survivors of their dignity and self-worth. This book affirms my hope that we will soon be able to live in a culture that accepts suicide as a normal reaction to chronic and severe depression, hopelessness and the overwhelming and unbearable mental and emotional pain that my daughter experienced.

Dr. Terence Barrett's book is about the grief and pain that survivors experience. For me, reading this book has at times been emotional, yet personally enlightening. It speaks to the fact that eventually we will find our way through the darkness, and while there may always be a tinge of sadness, there will come a sense of our own inner strength and our ability to rejoice in the life we have shared. We will begin to see a future in which the loved one, though not physically present, continues to bless us. Reading Life After Suicide will help those who grieve move with resoluteness and courage in gathering hope along the long road to recovery and reclamation of life.

Mary J. Weiler, Board Chair
North Dakota Chapter
American Foundation for Suicide Prevention
Survivor of Suicide Loss

Life After Suicide: The Survivor's Grief Experience

Preface

This book provides a description of the experience of survivors after suicidal death: of their struggles to deal with suicide and incorporate it into their own personal life histories, and of their efforts to reconstruct their lives in its aftermath. The material presented here is based on the growing literature about suicide survivorship and on interviews of survivors of suicide, accident, homicide, and natural death bereavements.

The impact of suicide, as in any death, most assuredly varies depending on the type and closeness of the relationship lost. For example, the experience of a wife whose husband completes suicide will be different in many important ways from a father whose son takes his own life. Although the impact of a suicide is greatly determined by the closeness of the relationship that had been formed with the decedent, no one associated with this form of death can escape its effects, regardless of distance from the deceased. Suicide touches something deep in the core of our humanness, and we can, none of us, be neutral to its occurrence.

Among the adult survivors who shared their experiences with me were fathers and mothers, husbands and wives, daughters and sons, sisters and brothers, and "just" friends and lovers. By far, a majority of the survivors had been spouses or parents of the deceased. Throughout the text, comments derived from their interviews are printed in "quotation marks" without their names. For purposes of anonymity, all direct survivor comments are noted to be from *A Survivor*, unless otherwise cited.

Not surprisingly, all suicide survivors do not share the same grief experiences. Every survivor experiences death in a unique style, and no one is likely to encounter the entire array of grief reactions presented in the following chapters. On the other hand, most adult suicide survivors, regardless of relationship to the deceased, will identify with much of the experience described here.

My hope in completing *Life After Suicide* is that it will provide insight into suicide survivorship, not only for those who experience, first hand, another person's self-destructive act, but also for those who interact with the survivors in the aftermath of the death. Survivors would find it a blessing if people they encountered after the experience of a suicide were more understanding and sensitive to their concerns.

one

Suicide: A Way of Dying

"Once every minute, or even more often, someone in the United States either kills himself or tries to kill himself with conscious intent. Sixty or seventy times every day these attempts succeed."
Karl A. Menninger [1]

Suicide. Self-inflicted, deliberate, and intentional death. It is one of four ways life officially ends in the United States. Accident, homicide, and natural cause are the other three ways.

Today, in our nation, suicide is considered among the ten leading causes of death; it is the fourth leading cause of death among adults, ages 18–65, and the second leading cause of death among teens, young adults, and college students. Suicide rates are highest among the 45–54 age group. Once an individual passes the age of 65, the risk of self-inflicted death increases. On average, our elderly adults complete nearly twenty percent of the suicides each year and more than 80% of those are by elderly males. Everywhere, death by suicide outnumbers homicides. Yet, when considering suicide on an individual basis, it does not discriminate among sex, race, creed, nationality, intelligence, health, social or economic status, success level, occupation, marital status, or age.

Statistics regarding this official form of death are widely and readily available, but are somewhat troublesome. Depending on the information source, suicide can be considered relatively rare or frighteningly common. Some professionals, citing rates like one suicide per every 10,000 people in the United States, view suicide as a rare event. Others view this act of self-destruction as endemic within our society, offering numbers varying anywhere between 30,000 to 50,000 suicidal deaths per year. Some experts, like Robert M. Hirschfeld and L. Davidson believe as many as ten times the number of people officially reported kill themselves each year. [2] About four percent of our population attempts to complete suicide every year. Estimates of total annual suicide attempts reach into the millions.

What Karl Menninger said about attempts and successful suicides in 1957 is now an underestimate. In the more than forty years after the end of World War II, the numbers of suicides continued to rise. By 1990, rates among young men had tripled and among young women had doubled. Today, one person dies by suicide in the United States every 13.7 minutes. Suicide claims more than 105 lives every day and an average of more than 38,000 lives each year. Attempts to die are reported every minute, amounting to nearly one million people attempting suicide annually.

Regardless of a person's stance on the prevalence of suicide within our society, it should cause concern to think that the names of individuals who kill themselves would, in one or two years' time, easily fill the Vietnam veterans war memorial, that respectfully and somberly lists the names of those killed in the entire course of the Vietnam War.

The difficulty with suicide statistics is that they are, by the very nature of the act, incomplete. This difficulty results from two factors, how suicide is defined and how it is reported.

Official definitions of suicide require that death must occur due to the deliberate intention and self-inflicted completion of a person's wish to die. Yet, in many deaths the intent of the victim to die is not clear and must, therefore, remain undetermined. For example, in some cases when the decedent intended to end his life, the death might appear accidental, as in a single-car automobile accident. In other cases, the intent on the decedent's part to die might have been absent, although the death appears to be a suicide. This might be true of some gunshot wounds self-inflicted during handling of a weapon and of some homicides that look like, or are made to look like, suicides. In deaths such as these, the victim's intent to die is not completely, or undeniably, obvious. Regardless of how these deaths are officially listed, they remain "equivocal deaths" (meaning a death difficult to interpret) in terms of cause.

In addition to equivocal deaths, the true extent of self-inflicted death is concealed by various prejudices surrounding the reporting of suicides. Reporting a suicide is a difficult matter, especially for those closest to the event.

Family members are particularly and understandably sensitive about social attitudes toward suicide. Dealing with the implications inherent in a suicide often takes a tremendous emotional toll on the family. Protecting themselves and the memory of the decedent can be a serious concern. It should not be surprising, then, that family members sometimes hide the suicidal nature of the death, if at all possible.

Medical and police officials can be sensitive to the hardships suicide brings to a family. They will sometimes report the death as an accident if the true nature of the death can be concealed. Furthermore, there are religious and bureaucratic complications that arise with a suicidal death. These often make it easier to label a death accidental or equivocal when possible. Finally, differences in coroners' procedures and post mortem examinations regarding the findings of equivocal deaths make the distinction between accident and suicide neither consistently clear nor painlessly reported. Many coroners will list a death as accidental or equivocal, even if the evidence leans more heavily toward suicide.

The numbers of suicides reported in our country are already worthy of our serious consideration. Yet, it is likely that the many prejudices regarding suicide and the equivocal nature of many deaths result in understatement of the number of annual suicides.

Who performs this act called suicide?

The question is often asked, in many ways. Who is most likely to suicide? Is this particular suicide unusual? Can a suicide be predicted? Who is most at risk? Researchers have been examining questions like these for decades.

As stated above, suicide does not discriminate among sex, race, creed, nationality, intelligence, health, social status, occupation, marital status, or age. It can occur anywhere. Sometimes it comes as a surprise, other times not. However, particular segments within our population *do* have higher rates of suicide than the overall national average and are considered at greater risk. Ronald Maris stated in 1981 that the greatest number of suicides occurred among physically ill, disabled or retired, and socially isolated older men. [3] Men historically have been at greater risk than women. Currently, nearly four men perform suicide for every one woman, although there is evidence that the number of women taking their own lives continues to increase.

The great number of news, magazine and research articles published since 2004 are indicative of the efforts to identify or predict those most likely to take their own lives. Included among at-risk individuals are: chronically depressed men and women; divorced, separated, or widowed elderly males; men dealing with chronic alcoholism; teenagers bullied by classmates; Native Americans living on reservations; Lesbian, Gay, Bisexual and Transgender individuals; and men serving in the military during the ongoing wars in Iraq and Afghanistan, particularly in the Army and the Marine Corps.

The relationship between depression related to neurochemical imbalances and suicide is unquestionable. Estimates from years of research suggest that 60% of the individuals who died by suicide were depressed. Compared to the risk in the general population, depressed individuals are fifty times more likely to die a self-inflicted death. The relationship between alcoholism and suicide is even greater. Suicide occurs 50% to 70% more often among those struggling with the ravages of alcoholism than it does in the general population.

During a decade of war, military suicides increased at a record rate, and attempted suicides rose every year. The numbers proved to be higher than the civilian suicide rates. Between 2005 and 2009, a total of 3,822 military fatalities were recorded in the theaters of war: 3,036 in Iraq and 786 in Afghanistan (see icasualties.org for all the names and statistics). In those five years, more than 1,100 military members killed themselves, equating to one suicide for every 3.5 service members killed. That also meant that another 6,600 survivors were trying to come to terms with self-inflicted death. In June 2010, a one-month record of thirty-two military suicides was reported.[4] Another 192 survivors in that one month received a call that their serviceman had died, a casualty of an internal war.

Incredible as it might seem, the only age group apparently exempt from suicidal death is children under the age of five, even though self-inflicted death has been officially reported among children as young as three years. Generally speaking, suicide seems most likely among men and women between the ages of thirty-five and sixty.

Among our nation's adolescents, 5,000 to 6,500 lives are lost annually to suicide—the second most common cause of death within this group. Only automobile accidents outrank suicide in killing our youth. Approximately 1,000 teenagers attempt suicide each day, and once every ninety minutes another young person succeeds. Quite alarmingly, the number of suicides that occurred among youths between ages 15–24 tripled in the 1970s and 1980s. In 2010, 2,546 suicides were recorded in that age group. In that same year, the elderly 65-years and older accounted for 5,987 suicides. The highest rate of completed suicides within the young population tends to be among the 18-year-olds about to attend college.

There are more suicide attempts than actual completions. In fact, nonfatal suicide attempts occur between six and eight times more often than completed suicides. Women who attempt suicide, but fail, outnumber men three to one.

That suicide attempts do not always succeed suggests that people who attempt to kill themselves, but fail, and people who succeed in completing suicide might be two different types of individuals. Evidence for this includes the fact that some individuals attempt suicide several times without ever successfully bringing their lives to an end. Ronald Maris estimated that 80% to 90% of those who attempt suicide sometime during their lives ultimately die non-suicidal deaths. On the other hand, 75% of the individuals who complete suicide are believed to have done so on their first attempt.

Care providers and families are alarmed that suicidal deaths seem to be on the rise. This increase is often attributed to various factors within our contemporary society. Such cause-and-effect statements require close scrutiny, however, and should be considered with caution. For one thing, instead of an ever-steady incline from prior periods, the number of suicides actually varies from one time to another. Large-scale phenomena like war, famine, and the state of the world economy affect suicide rates. Therefore, suicide rates go up and down over a long period of time.

Spikes in suicide rates *have* been noted in times of intense financial and personal stress. The Centers for Disease Control and Prevention report on suicide rates released in May 2013 highlighted dramatic elevations in suicides in the population among adults born between 1946 and 1960 (the Baby Boomers). From 1999 to 2010, the greatest increases in the U.S. occurred among men ages 50 to 54-years (up 49.4%) and ages 55 to 59-years (up 47.8%) and for women ages 60 to 64-years (up 59.7%).

Although social factors without doubt somehow influence suicide rates, they do not necessarily directly cause self-inflicted death. Most assuredly, contemporary social factors are not the root cause of suicide. Self-inflicted death has been a reality since mankind has made written records of its history. The act of suicide can be traced as far back as ancient Greek and Egyptian cultures and is described in the Bible no fewer than six times—interestingly, without hint of sanction or judgment. Throughout mankind's history, there have been times and there have been societies in which the act of suicide was openly accepted and was perceived without disdain, disgust, or disquiet. In fact, it is likely that there has never been a human culture or a time period in which self-inflicted death did not occur.

In light of such facts, it seems inappropriate to focus primarily on modern social phenomena in the study of suicide's cause. The attention really belongs upon the individuals who complete suicide. It might very well be more realistic to look upon suicide as a characteristic of being human, like sexuality, aging, and ultimately, mortality. This is not a new concept. Others, like Sigmund Freud, have wondered if self-destructive drives that actively oppose the instinct to survive and prosper might not be deeply buried within the psychological makeup of each individual. Everyone has likely met someone they would describe as "self-destructive." A person who seems to seek early fulfillment of a "death-wish" stands out in any crowd. Yet, these are the more obvious examples. There are other human behaviors that are not such blatant expressions of self-destructiveness.

A soldier's cradling himself around a grenade to save his comrades is understandably sentimentalized as a grand gesture of heroic proportions. That is only one respectful perspective, however. In terms of self-preservation and survival, this act could also be considered an extraordinary breakdown in the instinct to prolong one's life to a natural conclusion. We can look closer than this example for self-destructive behaviors. In fact, no individual acts instinctively in his or her own best behalf at all times.

There are times when we just do not take very good care of ourselves. This might take various forms like not eating nutritiously, having poor sleeping habits, overworking, abusing narcotics, smoking, drinking, or eating too much, driving dangerously, taking risks, and indulging in sexual promiscuity, to name just a few. Are these to be considered breakdowns in our human tendency and drive to survive? On an even more personal level, a great many people not outwardly self-destructive have, at one time or another, considered suicide for themselves. The majority of people have probably at least wondered what it would be like to bring about their own death.

It is safe to say that all individuals have entertained self-destructive thoughts, acts, or behaviors at different times in their lives. This suggests that self-destructive drives, though more apparent in some people than in others, do seem to be an ingrained part of our humanness. If this is a fact, it makes more sense to search for the meaning of suicide within individuals than it does within the social fabric of our contemporary culture.

The Study of Suicide

The reflective and investigative attention of modern scientific research has often been turned toward suicide. Professionals have made great efforts to understand, deter, and prevent suicide in their investigation of suicide. They have undertaken to discover whether or not suicide is a result of a genetic inheritance. They have studied character traits and personalities to see if certain ones might make a person especially prone to suicide.

During this investigative search, psychological autopsies have been performed on the lives of those who have completed suicide. Differences between people who actually succeed at suicide and those who merely attempt it have been studied. Speculation about the hidden motives for self-destruction continues to captivate the attention of many researchers. External factors believed by some to lead to suicide have also been studied. Even the many, varied, and imaginative ways people inflict death upon themselves have been investigated.

Without question, research has resulted in a growing understanding of the self-destructive human tendency. However, neither the prevention of suicide nor a reduction in the numbers of people who choose suicide as their way of ending life have been achieved.

This raises a question regarding the utility and effectiveness of prevention and intervention centers located in many communities. While some research demonstrates the influence these centers have exerted in saving individual lives, other studies suggest suicide prevention services have had little impact upon reducing the frequency of suicides within any community.

The Samaritan organization provides an example. The Samaritans are a group of trained, nonsectarian laymen in the British Isles who volunteer their "friendship" to individuals experiencing a suicidal crisis. The impact the Samaritans have had in communities they serve has been so widely lauded that Samaritan branches have been organized in many other countries, including the United States. Yet, studies of the Samaritans' overall effectiveness in reducing suicide rates have been disappointing. Again, although the volunteers have proved very effective in thwarting the self-destructive urges of many individuals on a course toward suicide, they have been unable to either prevent or reduce the occurrence of suicide within their communities.

Additionally, the human motivation for self-destruction has not been, and most assuredly cannot be, eliminated from the human psyche. If an individual chooses to end his own life, for whatever reason, there are enough opportunities and enough lethal methods available for him to do so. When a person's own suicidal intent overwhelms him, it seems no amount of intervention, love, or caring will ultimately deter him from a self-destructive course. For this reason alone, preventing suicide within our culture assumes impossible proportions.

This is not to say that professionals working in the field have failed. They have made progress and met with successes. Through their diligent labors, effective methods of dealing with individuals in a suicidal crisis have been developed. Indeed, there are many people alive today who would otherwise have successfully ended their lives were it not for the concerned intervention of others employing such methods. However, predicting which individual, at which time, and under which circumstances will complete suicide remains nearly impossible. The opportunity to activate crisis intervention methods, therefore, does not always occur.

Three organizations in particular in the United States have dedicated their efforts to preventing suicides with significant, and various, impact. The one best known by the general population is the national Crisis Center/Hotline, with more than 150 service centers found in community telephone directories under Suicide Intervention listings.

The second is the American Association of Suicidology (AAS), a not-for-profit organization founded in 1968 with the mission to understand and prevent suicide as a means of promoting a sense of well being for all humans.

As part of its commitment to reducing the number of suicides and suicide attempts, public education and information have become core functions of the AAS. The organization collects fact sheets, national suicide statistics and current research studies on suicide and produces a variety of brochures, reports, books, and resources. In addition to suicide prevention activities, the AAS also sponsors a *Healing After Suicide* conference each year to share suicide bereavement information to both professionals and survivors and publishes its *Surviving Suicide* newsletter in order to circulate supportive information to suicide survivors and the professionals who work with them. (See the AAS Web site at Suicidology.org.)

The third influential organization was founded in 1987. The American Foundation for Suicide Prevention (AFSP) is a not-for-profit organization dedicated exclusively to preventing suicide. The AFSP has become the nation's leading organization in the effort to understand and prevent suicide and to help heal the pain self-inflicted death causes to survivors. Having established more than fifty local chapters in thirty-five states, the AFSP brings together and galvanizes individuals, families, and communities personally affected by suicide and funds research, education and treatment programs. Specific AFSP activities are described further in Chapter Ten. (See, also, the AFSP Web site at afsp.org.)

Can We Ever Accept Suicide?

Acceptance is a word meaning a willingness to believe that something is true, a tolerance without protest, and a coming to terms with an indisputable fact. Acceptance is an attitude that emerges from careful thought.

Theorists and practitioners within the profession of suicide prevention have developed a special insight regarding suicide. Though they continue to work to save the lives of people entangled in self-destructive careers, they accept the obvious fact that suicide has not been eliminated from the human experience and that it probably will never be "preventable." They do not necessarily consider suicide as an acceptable death, but they do accept that suicides will occur beyond all efforts invested in stopping them. They do not like the fact that suicides happen, but they accept that they do. In this, these individuals appear to have come to terms with the act of suicide.

There is wisdom in accepting that suicides will occur no matter what external circumstances appear to be in any person's life. Proof that social factors cause or prevent suicide is lacking. Although external social factors contribute to a person's choice to complete suicide, such factors are not the sole cause of self-destructive acts. In fact or fantasy, social engineers might structure a society someday in which the supposed factors influencing self-destructive actions are nonexistent, but it is doubtful any scientific endeavor will ever completely eliminate the human drive for self-destruction.

Where there are humans, there will likely be suicide. But, does that make suicide an acceptable form of death in our society?

Understanding Suicide and its Impact is an upper level university course offering an overview of our current understanding of suicide dynamics and of its impact upon people left behind following the death. [5] The objectives are for students to develop familiarity with the experience of suicide in contemporary America and to increase understanding of the impact suicide has upon family members and society. Most of the students across twelve years, from

2002 to 2013, and thirty-six semesters were juniors and seniors, with a few sophomores and graduate students also registered for the course. Although the students represented a wide array of studies, the greatest proportion were psychology, criminal justice, counseling, and nursing majors.

"Would you argue for the belief that death by suicide is normal? What points would you offer to support your opinion?" are the final two questions the students are asked to address in the course. Many students acknowledged that this was a difficult issue to answer. A small portion left the question unanswered. Others were undecided, seeing it in both ways, stating that they could neither advocate nor oppose suicide as a normal death. Some insisted that the idea of normal is determined by society, not by the nature of things, and that normal is what is acceptable to the majority or to "the powers that be." Death is normal, and categorizing it into "normal" and "not normal" is counter-productive to dealing with it. They would not view it as a taboo and would not "condone" it.

Of the 644 students who argued an opinion for one or the other, 283 (an encouraging 44%) believed that death in all forms, including suicide, is a normal part of life. Many of the students who had come to accept suicide as a normal death had experienced the suicide of a loved one in their lives. The points they offered to support their view tended to be short, straight forward, and repeated across the twelve years.

* The person could not deal with life stresses.
* They are in unbearable pain.
* Depression and mental illness are the cause and they are no different than cancer or other fatal illnesses.
* Suicide is normal response to chronic and severe depression.
* The cause can be a biological imbalance, a neurobiological imbalance, or a neuro-chemical imbalance.
* Death is normal no matter what kind it is or how it happens.

* The majority of people don't have a practical view of death and can't see that suicide is normal.
* Suicide is a universal human experience, so it must be normal.
* It is just another form of death.
* Death is inevitable for everyone.
* Making something right or wrong, even death, is an unfair judgment.
* It is selfish and self-centered to judge another person's choice as bad.
* Social norms are subjective and change over time. That means suicide is not inherently abnormal.
* Religious views judge suicide unfairly.
* Suicide is caused by a predisposed condition that the person has no control over. It's probably inevitable for many who die this way.

The points offered by 361 students (56%) to support their view that suicide was not normal and should not be accepted by society tended to be longer responses and far more varied. Their points are introduced later in Chapters Seven and Eight.

One premise developed in this book is that the true weight of social factors does not fall upon people who contemplate or complete suicide. Certainly, social influences definitely have no impact upon the decedent once the act has been completed. The real power of contemporary social factors in regard to suicide is upon the people left behind by the suicide. Current social perceptions, beliefs, attitudes, and conventions have a significant influence primarily upon the experience of survivors in the aftermath of a suicide.

This chapter, about the act of suicide and those who choose to perform it is simply an introduction to an experience that affects millions of lives. Among the four recognized ways of dying in our society, suicide is emphatically different from the other forms of death.

It is different because in this single method of death, there is a seemingly obvious choice to die. It is different because there is generally a message conveyed to the survivors that implies more than just the decedent's wish to die. It is different because its performance causes discomfort, disgust, and disquiet within the general society. And, finally, it is different because our present social institutions and conventions typically provide no constructive structures to facilitate or ease the survivor's grief.

How the differences inherent within suicidal death impact the survivors is the heart of this book. Hopefully, greater insights about the experience of suicide's survivors will result in more sensitive perceptions of suicide. Surprisingly perhaps, it is the survivors who will profit from a more enlightened acceptance of suicide's realities.

Enlightenment allows, rather then prevents, more gentle expression of our humanness. Today, social and moral issues are generally in a process of revision. Former taboos and sanctions are being more widely and more closely scrutinized. In this analysis, they are losing some of their power to frighten and to inhibit. Examples of issues with which our maturing society wrestles include the continuing and growing controversies over abortion, euthanasia (assisted suicide), capital punishment, gun control, and nuclear armament. The dilemma of suicide belongs among these social and moral issues.

Moral, legal, and medical questions involving a person's right to choose method and time of death are currently under debate and discussion in open forums. The September 1989 decision of a Georgia Superior Court Judge to allow a paralyzed civil engineer to end his own life by removing himself from life-sustaining medical equipment serves as an example. It is evident that opinions among religious, professional, and public domains about these concerns are being challenged and are changing.

Although neither to be encouraged nor condoned, suicide might be accepted in the future as an act that humans perform, just like it was sometimes viewed in the past. It will not be considered a crime, sin, weakness, mental illness, pathology, failure, or comment against the social and human condition and will not elicit feelings of disgust, disdain, or shame.

If the debate over suicide is ever resolved, suicide might become a preferred way of dying for some people, much as it was in other societies in other times. Michael C. Kearl and Richard Harris believed the emerging attitudes toward death in our country include the consideration of a person's right to control the form and timing of his or her death.[6] Perhaps by having a choice regarding the time and method of one's own death, by freely and openly dealing with the human motivation for self-destruction, and by thus coming face-to-face with the reality that death awaits us all, we would all be better able to accept our humanness and the responsibilities for life that are as much a part of being human as are the opposing drives for survival and self-destruction.

Understanding the connections between social views and attitudes toward suicide and the trauma that survivors after self-inflicted death encounter is an important matter. Any change in the way suicide is perceived and accepted will directly influence the grief experiences of these survivors. The remainder of this book presents a discussion of the impact of suicide and the survivor's bereavement.

two

The Grieving Survivor

> *"Pain is my constant companion. Everywhere I go, it demands my attention, even in my dreams."*
>
> A Survivor

"Survivor" is a common and familiar name. It is often assigned to people who are left behind after another dies. Obituaries name survivors. The media, professionals and clergy frequently phrase bereavement in terms of survivorship. For example, "He is survived by his wife, Mary Ellen, and his two daughters, Pamela and Amy," or more simply, "Survivors include his wife and two daughters" are both expressions of the concept of survivorship following a death. The common use of "survivor" obscures how appropriately it describes the experience of those in the decedent's life. A survivor does more than continue to live on after the decedent's death. He or she actually survives the death. He or she suffers through and *survives* a bereavement.

During the emotional and traumatic experience of grieving, the life of the survivor is, in many ways, at risk. There is the chance he might not survive at all, but might become a fatality himself somewhere in the aftermath of the death. Therefore, when the death is sufficiently past and the bereavement is finished, the individual left behind has truly traveled in harm's way and survived. Bereavement after death is passage to a new life, sometimes better and sometimes worse. It is a survivorship. This chapter now turns to the description of survivorship following suicide.

Suicide is sometimes perceived as an intensely private and personal act, as if a person's choice to end her own, single life affects only her. Sadly, this is never true. In most cases, suicide is an event that at least involves relatives and friends. Tensions that result in a self-destructive course are almost invariably between two people, whether that be husband and wife, parent and child, or boyfriend and girlfriend. Even suicides that appear to be completely isolated do not take place in social or interpersonal vacuums. Someone must discover the suicide's body. Sometimes paramedics, emergency room personnel, or physicians become involved in futile life-saving efforts. Someone must notify officials of the suicidal nature of the death. Officials must file reports. The coroner, mortician, cemetery personnel, and often times the media get involved. If the media brings attention to the suicide, many people without knowledge, contact, or emotional investment involving the decedent must deal with the suicide.

No one has a neutral reaction to a suicide—an act seemingly able to squeeze strong emotions from each of us. When we have news even of a distant, unknown death by suicide, it can shock and trouble us. Suicide is rejection on the highest scale. Perhaps the person who takes her own life turns her back, in the most extreme manner, upon our society. In the aftermath we question the value of the lives we have made for ourselves. And when we question life, anxieties regarding death are awakened. Dealing with another person's suicide, then, turns to reflection upon the meaning of our own lives and inevitable deaths.

The reaction to suicide might have roots deeper than we realize. Quite possibly the emotions unearthed by suicide are not even developed in our own lifetimes. It has been suggested that there is buried within each of us a primitive fear or superstition about death that suicide releases from the shadowy caverns of our unconscious. Does suicide breathe life to an ancestral fear that a dead person extracts some vengeance from those who have been left behind? Whatever the roots of the reaction to it, suicide unquestionably extracts a terrible vengeance upon the survivors. The extent of this vengeance upon those left behind is described in the following chapters.

Gerald P. Ginsburg conducted a study in Reno, Nevada, investigating public conceptions and attitudes about suicide that helps grasp how widespread the impact of suicide is in our culture.[7] Of the people he interviewed, 74% knew one or more persons who had either completed suicide, attempted suicide, or probably attempted suicide. Fifty-three percent personally knew at least one person who had completed suicide. Of these, 21% were family members of the decedent, 37% knew the decedent very well, and another 29% knew the decedent at least fairly well.

Skeptics might rightfully doubt statistics gathered from a single study carried out in one location, especially one like Reno which might be accused of attracting a certain kind of person. There are other studies, however, that indicate the enormity of suicide's influence. Edwin Shneidman, for example, estimated that the number of family members who survive suicide is between 250,000 and 300,000 annually.[8] Over a period of years, this number swells into the millions. The number of people, including family, friends, and associates who are intimately associated with suicide might be as high as 750,000 a year.

Shneidman postulated that every one suicide leaves behind at least six survivors.[9] In the course of a few years, the number of people who must deal with the impact of suicide becomes staggering. Alan L. Berman, collected data from 1983 to 2009 and, using Shneidman's conservative estimate, put the number of suicide survivors in the U.S. at about 4.73 million. Approximately 221,454 suicide survivors joined that number in 2009.[10]

Those with a philosophic outlook seem to accept that a person who dies has left suffering behind. It is the survivor who must deal with the aftermath of death. Whether or not our entire population is touched on some emotional level by each individual report of suicide, it is evident that millions of people are coping with this self-destructive act on an intimate basis. It is the grieving survivor closest to the suicide who must suffer the trauma of loss. As, Louis Wekstein said, in the matter of suicide it is the survivor who is the true victim. [11]

The Suicide Survivor as Victim

Historically, the survivor was not always victimized by someone else's suicide. In times past and in cultures long expired, suicide was not considered sick, deviant or criminal. In ancient Greek, Roman, and Norse cultures, and in not so ancient asian cultures, taking one's life was looked upon as a noble act in many instances. In fact, there were circumstances under which suicide might he dictated by social pressures or custom. These cultures permitted a person to find an honorable solution to many dishonorable or intolerable situations through suicide. To perform suicide was to act honorably and to lend pride to the person's name and memory. The act itself did not necessarily conjure up reactions of fear, shame, or blame nor did it inspire legal punishment, degradation, or revenge.

Socrates is not the only famous person to have selected his own death. There are numerous other names recorded in history of those who chose suicide as the preferred method of death, including King Saul, Demosthenes, Mark Antony, Cleopatra, Brutus and Hannibal.

The social acceptability of suicide was altered drastically and with far-reaching social impact in the sixth century, C.E. (A.D.). The victimization of the survivor can be traced at least back to that century. Largely as a reaction to the widespread quest for martyrdom undertaken by the early Christians, especially the Zealots, St. Augustine spoke out against suicide and the deliberate engineering of one's own death. Afterwards, in 533 C.E. (A.D.), the Church decreed that suicide was the most deadly of all mortal sins. In the words of Alfred Alvarez, "an act which during the first flowering of Western civilizations had been tolerated, later admired, and later still sought as the supreme mark of zealotry, became finally the object of intense moral revulsion." [12]

At that point in our social history, the persecution of the survivor became sanctioned on religious grounds and from that historical moment to the present day, the consequences for suicide have been borne by the survivor, not the decedent. Damning a soul to hell or refusing consecrated burial has little impact upon the decedent after the self-destructive act has been completed. The survivor, however, experiences both the worry and concern for the soul of the departed and the hardships and stigma of severely altered funeral and burial practices that, from ancient times, have been designed to ease the sting of death for the bereaved.

Victimization of the survivor received legal sanctification later. In Europe, a person who performed suicide was labeled either a criminal or a lunatic. In either case, the state was legally justified in taking the suicide's property for its own. In this fashion, the family survivors were both cheated of any inheritance due them and were stigmatized by the suspicion of genetically transmitted lunacy. The laws supporting the victimization of the survivors held on until recent generations. For example, the laws in England permitting the confiscation of a suicide's property were not revised until the late 1800s.

It is important to understand the influence of the religious and legal sanctions imposed upon suicide. The cost or penalty of suicide could not be borne by the person who performed the so-called "sin" or "crime." After all, the sinner or criminal was no longer at hand, and the long arm of the law can reach only so far. The consequences, or better still, the punishments for the suicide, if they were to be meted out, had to fall upon the heads of those left behind. In times past those punishments included cruel burial practices, the collection of taxes, the leveling of fines, and the confiscation of property. Beyond the obvious losses, the survivor eventually was seen to somehow share the responsibility for an act in which he had no hand. He became guilty and, therefore, punished for an association with the decedent.

In times present, the circumstances are changed only on the surface of the issue. No longer is the survivor taxed, fined, or cheated of property, except perhaps in the matter of insurance policy payments. Today, the survivor pays the penalty for another's suicide in a more subtle and, perhaps, more devastating manner. The punishments for suicide today are largely emotional and psychological.

Many contemporary researchers believe the impact of suicide far exceeds that of any other form of death. This is especially true for the family of a person who chooses to end her own life. The surviving family finds it exceptionally difficult to understand the suicidal act of one of its members. The emotional consequences of such an event have been known to endure for excessive periods of time. Louis Wekstein believes that the presence of a person dead by suicide lingers on, festering and hounding the lives of the family and others associated with him long after the decedent's departure. The survivors abruptly left behind endure emotions that might never end or be resolved.

✳ ✳ ✳

"The lifelong grief and disruptions [suicide] causes
in other people's lives are unspeakable."

Suzanne Gerber [13]

✳ ✳ ✳

After any death, survivors experience what is called a grief process. Using the word "process" implies that grief involves a number of particular actions, or reactions, and that it continues over a period of time. The manner in which the process of grieving progresses has been studied widely, and many grief reactions have been recognized.

In many ways, the suicide grief process has features in common with other bereavements. In other ways, suicide bereavement is different from other bereavements in important aspects, for it is also comprised of grief reactions that are rare in non-suicidal deaths.

The next chapter begins the description of the grief experience as suicide survivors encounter it.

three

The Grief Complex

"In the apportionment of suffering, the sting of death is always less sharp for the person who dies than it is for the survivor."
Arnold J. Toynbee [14]

The sting of death comes in a common and consistent form among all humans. It is a process called grieving, or sometimes mourning or bereaving. Though this process has many different components in various cultures, it is an experience that is shared by all people who have suffered through the death of someone intimately known to them. Before going on to a description of grief following suicide, it is helpful to first discuss some general concepts about grieving.

Our first impressions of grieving are formed by observing others in grief. As children, we might be witness to adults in our lives grieving. We view grief vicariously on television. We hear other people talk of grief. Even as adults, we continue to learn about and be witness to grief. For example, we might know friends who experience the death of a parent or friend. We watch their grief and might intellectually understand it, but emotionally we can little comprehend its full impact.

Observing someone else's grief merely provides a lesson in grief behavior, but does not prepare us for the experience of our own grief. We might learn how people act when they are grieving, but very few of us are sensitive enough to know what a person is feeling when she grieves. Until it is experienced first hand, grief is something that can only be imagined. And, because so much of grieving is solitary, private, internal, and unobservable, what we view of another's grief is not preparation enough for the personal experience of it. Therefore, a person who has never experienced the death of someone close is likely to be terribly surprised, if not frighteningly overwhelmed, by the intimate encounter with grief.

* * *

"Well, everyone can master grief, but he who has it."

William Shakespeare [15]

* * *

Grieving is a natural, human process that occurs with the experience of significant loss, especially that of a loved person. In his description of grief, Edwin Shneidman suggested that the bereaved survivor is likely to be affected as if she were suffering from a disease of known course. "The recently bereaved person is typically bereft and disorganized. Longstanding habit patterns of intimate interpersonal responses are irreversibly severed. There is a concomitant gale of strong feelings, usually including abandonment and despair, sometimes touching upon guilt and anger, and almost always involving a sense of crushing emptiness and loss. There might be serious physical and psychological [features] in the way of heightened morbidity and even greater risk of death." [16]

The experience of grief can be viewed as a combination of two different and somewhat opposing processes. The first process is often referred to as separation or detachment from the deceased. The second is commonly called reconstruction or recovery. While each of these processes is believed to serve a specific purpose for the bereaved, in combination, the dual processes of separation and reconstruction, make up what is commonly called the "grief process."

Separation

Generally, the purpose of the grief process is to enable a person to first separate from the lost loved one and then to reconstruct a life that no longer includes that important person.

The process of separation from the deceased is indicated by the emotional expression of pain, of suffering, of loss. This process embodies the traditional concept of grief and becomes active immediately upon having knowledge of the death. This is the process around which most funeral rites are structured. Through its expression, both the survivor and society acknowledge that death has brought a terrible loss to those left behind.

During the course of separation, others accept that the grieving survivor will not be herself for a period of time. Her actions and reactions will also be expected to be different from before the death. In fact, some behaviors considered out-of-the-ordinary in normal daily interactions are actually expected during grieving. Examples include crying, wailing, incessant talking or oppressive silence, irrationality, obsession with death, breaking or throwing objects, wandering aimlessness or blunted inactivity, and hyper-alertness.

The underlying function of this initial process is gradual separation from the deceased. Even when the death can be consciously acknowledged, or evidently known in a person's awareness, the survivor will unconsciously try to hold on to, or bring back the lost loved one. Initially, then, the function of grief is to help the survivor detach emotionally from the deceased. If detachment does not occur, the survivor will cling both emotionally and psychologically to the deceased.

In that case, the grief process becomes short-circuited. Additionally, if this first purpose of grief is not achieved, it will take longer for the second grief process to get underway. Recovery, if it gets started, also becomes less likely to be successfully completed.

Recovery

Reconstruction or recovery is the second process active within grieving. It is the process that brings the survivor back toward a meaningful and satisfying life.

The specific purpose of the reconstruction process is to redirect the survivor's emotional investment away from the decedent and toward other and/or new relationships. During this part of grieving, the survivor begins building a new life in which the decedent is no longer a present and significant feature. The outcome, then, can be a life that the survivor finds rewarding and full, and in which she can express love and trust freely.

Recovery obviously begins later in the grief process than separation, but the two are active together at some point. Recovery is marked by the gradual diminishing of the strong reactions that immediately follow death. As separation progresses, the survivor slowly learns to pace the process. A balance is gradually reached between grieving the loss of the loved one and participating in everyday life. Moments of severe grief become shorter-lasting and less frequent in occurrence. As Colin M. Parkes and Robert S. Weiss described, recovery from bereavement is typically marked by the absence of grief reactions, by the establishment, maintenance, and involvement in helpful and gratifying relationships, and by the achievement of a new quality of satisfaction in life. [17]

Ultimately, with time and efficient grieving, grief becomes a dull ache, a brief memory that now and then intrudes upon an otherwise adjusted life. Parkes and Weiss concluded that good recovery outcomes are characterized not only by adequate functioning in social roles and freedom from physical and emotional symptoms traceable to the grief, but also by emotional investment in the present life, by hope regarding the future, and by a return to a genuine capacity for experiencing gratification.

The Course Grieving Takes

As a process, grieving has an identifiable beginning, an expected course, a conceivable ending, and a purposeful, desirable outcome. Both time and energy are required of the survivor if the process is to be successful. Although both of these ingredients are available to the bereaved, neither of them should be taken for granted. Emotional and psychological malfunctions or de-railings are likely if the survivor tries to avoid, shortcut, abbreviate, or delay the grieving process. Grieving takes time and it must be rendered its due.

* * *

> "I tell others, 'Don't think there are any shortcuts.' It's like you did something really wrong, and you have to serve your time."
>
> A Survivor

* * *

A survivor cannot expect grieving to simply occur and then to be gone, like a wave washing over her on a beach. The survivor does not just stand in the way of grief and allow it to wash over her in its course. The grief process is functional only if the survivor provides concentrated effort that, then, supplies the energy to keep this natural process on a healthy course.

The processes of separation and recovery require a great expenditure of effort to accomplish completely. The survivor must work at grieving if the process is to succeed. The effort supplied is usually called the "grief work." This term implies that the survivor must do something in order to grieve.

Ideally, effective grief work would be powered by knowledge of the physical, emotional, psychological, and behavioral reactions to grief and how best to resolve them. In one sense, the need for such knowledge might seem superfluous. After all, grieving is so natural that it might be instinctual. However, the work required to accomplish grieving is not necessarily so natural.

The fact is, *how* we grieve is greatly determined by social and cultural directives, standards, and traditions. Unfortunately for the survivor, socially accepted methods for grieving are not necessarily the most effective ways of dealing with the inner turmoil that occurs. Therefore, though grieving effectively is a skill that could be learned, it is typically acquired only through on-the-job experience.

As in all things human, there is great variety in the expression of grief. This makes it difficult to speak in generalities about the course and duration of the grief process. There are, however, trends and consistencies that occur frequently enough to describe grief as an entity with possible limits.

The Stages of Grief

The literature on death and bereavement provides many fine descriptions of the process, course, and patterns of grief. Included among the most often-read treatments of the grief process are those of Erich Lindemann,[18] John Bowlby,[19] and Colin Parkes.[20] These authors describe the grief process as an observable sequence of events that can be divided into stages. In other words, there are particular things that happen during grieving and, in many instances, they occur within predictable time periods. Consequently, most authors divide the grief process into three or four distinct stages.

Typically, the stages of the grief process are given names like Immediate or Shock Phase, Intermediate or Disorganization Phase, and Final or Recovery Phase. These various stages are suggested to be common among most survivors during grieving and specific grief work is accomplished during each phase. However, a caution should always be added to viewing grief within the framework of stages. Stages are a convenient way for understanding the grief experience. They do not provide an exact description of grief's course. In reality, grieving is an ongoing process, not a series of stages marked by specific events, milestones, or timetables.

Grief stages do not realistically progress from one to the next in order. There is overlap in the activity of the stages. While the work of one stage is predominant, a little bit of the work of another might also be underway. Also, at a point when the survivor is primarily invested in the grief work of any particular stage, regressions and progressions from that stage to another are likely. For example, it is not unusual for a survivor involved in work of the later recovery stage to experience brief, temporary waves of the extreme sorrow first encountered in the initial grief period.

Unknown and unwritten conventions in our culture somewhat determine how long the grief process lasts. Our society allots a certain period of time in which the survivor is expected to accomplish the grief work. We might call this the "official grieving period." During this period, the behaviors and activities of grief are expected and condoned. This is the time when society says to the survivor, "Go ahead. We know your behavior is unusual and disturbing, but we will tolerate it because you are in grief." However, when grief behavior goes beyond the accepted cultural limits, it is usually perceived to be abnormal, unhealthy, deviant, or frightening. In many cases, if grief exceeds what is considered normal, the survivor will gradually be abandoned and isolated.

Time allotted to grieving has changed in our culture. In previous generations, the bereft wore black clothing, or at least a black armband to signal to others that bereavement was underway. A year spent grieving was considered customary and expected. Today's culture has shortened this significantly. Some employees are given three days off from work to attend memorial services and funerals and to attend to affairs. Then, they are expected to be back at work and to conduct themselves in a way that does not make coworkers uncomfortable.

* * *

> "It was about two months after my son overdosed. I had been back to the job for seven weeks. My supervisor called me into his office and asked if something was wrong. My annual performance review was coming and my work seemed sub-par to him."
>
> A Survivor

* * *

The individuals surrounding the grieved survivor are usually responsible for initiating the closure of the official grieving period. They somehow signal the survivor that there has been enough of grieving. Sometimes this signal is conveyed in a gentle, subtle manner. For example, most comforters patiently listen to the survivor's grief immediately after the death. With time, the willingness to listen to sorrowful lamenting might no longer be extended to the survivor.

People uncomfortably change the subject when the survivor tries to talk about the decedent. Also, fewer opportunities to call upon the survivor are taken as time passes. A friend might arrange activities to get her out socially.

The accepted period of grief is often ended by more obvious means than just described. Some survivors are openly berated by those close to them; harshly prodded to be done with their grief. Perhaps scolded that they have cried and carried on enough, they hear it is time to get on with their lives. They are told not to dwell so much on the past—the time has come to move on and to put the death and grief behind them. Remarks like "snap out of it" or "stop feeling sorry for yourself" or "is this all you ever think about" are not unusual. Such insensitive comments immediately signal survivors that people around them have had enough of their grief.

The process of grieving does not end when the comforters become uncomfortable with it and indicate that it is time for it to cease. By whatever means the signal to end the official mourning period is passed, from the survivor's perspective it comes too soon. The survivor typically would like more time to accomplish the overt grief work: more time to hold on to the deceased and the shared part of their lives. Grief usually goes on far longer than those around the survivor are willing or able to accept or tolerate. If the survivor is to ensure that those she needs do not abandon her, further alienating her from the comfort she desires, she must take the grief activity underground.

A survivor learns to put up a front, or at least to try to appear as if everything is generally good. Efforts at this point are directed at making sure others feel comfortable around her. Gradually, her interactions, demeanor, conversations, and behavior are brought in line with what others would like to see. Meanwhile, as she deliberately tries to "tough it out alone" or "put it in the past," in the underground recesses of the survivor's mind, body, and soul, the pain continues. The suffering goes on.

The sense of loss is not overcome. Grief becomes something internal to which the survivor must somehow respond and in some way resolve. In most cases, from this point on, the work of grief is carried out alone.

Survivors learn to grieve away from others. This is a dangerous development. Grief is like a scab forming over an open wound on its way to becoming a scar. If it is too soon repressed or too deeply buried beneath the gauze and wrappings of socially acceptable interactions and behavior, it can become a festering, easily opened wound. Such a wound has the potential to torment the survivor for the rest of her life. Grief must be opened to the light of day and the breath of fresh air, if the wounds of survivorship are to be healed, and the survivor is to become fully healthy.

That others signal the end of the official grieving period is not always the disservice to the survivor it might appear to be. It can be a benefit to the survivor if it does not occur prematurely or insensitively. Without external signals the survivor might wallow indefinitely in grief. This might in fact be what happens to unfortunate survivors who are isolated from social contact for some reason. Mired in grief, they have no signal or push to remove themselves from it. At some point the survivor can sink so deeply into grief that she is incapable of getting herself out without help. Comforters can, therefore, be instrumental in providing the initial impetus for both the separation and the reconstruction processes of grief. They are, however, only the catalysts. The survivor must always accomplish the real grief work.

Grief Reactions

The work of grief involves successfully managing and resolving the many reactions that arise after the experience of death. These reactions can be viewed as the elements or components of the grief process. Grief reactions are the things that survivors experience in the processing of their grief.

Many reactions to loss are readily observable to people around the survivor. Other grief reactions are basically internal states that are less obvious and more hidden from view, especially once the official grieving period has been closed.

Reactions to death are not the same in the experience of all survivors. While some reactions might be universal grief experiences, others are rarely encountered. Whether or not a reaction is activated and with what intensity is determined partly by the characteristics of the survivor and partly by the circumstances surrounding the death.

The components of grief experienced by survivors in our culture have been well documented and are described in other fine works. This book describes the grief reactions as they are experienced by a special group of survivors. In the following chapters, the reactions of those who have been subjected to the experience of someone else's suicidal action are explained.

Not Forgiven

Do you see me here all alone?
These thoughts in me are not my own
To suffer is to feel you know
And this will pass through me

Do you see me here on my own?
My life now is mine alone
This weight is one I've felt you know
And this will pass through me

When I leave you here all alone
Know these thoughts are not my own
To suffer is to feel you know
And this will pass through me
Oh God, let this pass through me

I am not forgiven
for what I did not do
I am not the devil
I only knew what I knew

Brenda Weiler
—
Survivor of Suicide Loss
Singer/Songwriter

four

The Tidal Wave After Suicide

> *"There are essentially only two kinds of mourning and grief and reconstitutive patterns: those which accrue by accident, disaster, homicide, and natural causes and those which relate to the stigmatizing death of a loved one by suicide."*
>
> Edwin Shneidman [21]

The suggestion seems reasonable that the grief reactions of survivors who were intimately associated with a person who died by suicide are qualitatively and quantitatively different from those resulting from other forms of death. For example, Edwin Shneidman stated that "the survivor of a suicidal death must recover psychologically on a different level from that of people who have suffered a more natural bereavement. Natural, accidental, or even homicidal deaths elicit deep feelings of loss, emptiness, sorrow, loneliness, disbelief, torment, yearning, anguish, and heartache; in the case of suicidal death, these emotions are intensified and aggravated, sometimes to unbearable proportions, by the grim additions of shame, guilt, self-blame, and hostility." [22]

Even individuals who have experienced a past bereavement in their lives show evidence that they are not prepared for the trauma and upheaval that accompanies a suicidal death. Shneidman suggested that suicide results in a grief far more intense than any other form of death.

Saying there are two patterns of grieving, those experienced by suicide survivors and those experienced by all other survivors, implies that suicide bereavement is unique. Is suicide bereavement really different from other forms of grieving? Do suicide survivors experience grief reactions unknown, unrecognizable, or incomprehensible to other survivors? Such questions are important to consider if we are to understand the grief experienced as a result of someone else's suicide.

It is intuitively and logically clear that, because suicide is a different sort of death, suicide survivorship is different in form and expression. However, before considering any further whether or not suicide bereavement is truly unique, three aspects are considered that make it likely to be different.

Suicide Is Unexpected

First of all, suicidal death is usually sudden and unexpected. In its swiftness, the survivor has typically not prepared for it. Even in relationships in which one has made comments about his/her intention to complete a suicidal act, or even has made previous attempts, others do not believe it will really happen. Accepting the possibility of a suicide seems initially, and naturally, beyond the capacities of a reasonable, rational, and realistic mind. Preparation for and anticipation of a death might be one of the most important determinants of the survivor's ability to accept the death of an intimate and of the adequacy of the recovery from it. Some researchers conclude that lack of preparation results in unexpected death being more difficult to grieve than death that has been anticipated. Parkes and Weiss, for example, suggested that unexpected death, regardless of its cause, occasions the most severe bereavement reactions. [23]

Suicide is a form of unexpected death. However, that the suicide survivor typically does not have the opportunity to anticipate or prepare for the death, completely explains neither the differences in suicide bereavement nor the impact of suicidal death upon the survivors. Even in instances in which the deceased was ill and death was expected, if death occurs because the ill person completes suicide, the survivor might experience a far more intense grief than would have been occasioned by the natural death.

A Prejudice Against Suicide

A second factor that contributes to the different nature of suicide bereavement is the fact that suicide seems to agitate deep emotional reactions even in people distantly removed from the decedent. It is likely that every individual in our society has deeply developed feelings, biases, or prejudices, against self-inflicted death—the reactions of others to suicide are seldom neutral. More than any other manner of death, suicide is likely to generate an almost instinctual reaction of repugnance, judgment, incrimination, blame, discomfort, confusion, hatred, anger, or denial.

The definition of *prejudice* includes two elements: 1) it is a preference based on a judgment for one thing over another, and 2) it is an unfavorable opinion or disdain toward the other, especially when the opinion has been formed prior to experience or without knowledge of the other. Does the concept of prejudice really fit when considering the experiences of suicide survivors? If it does, what does it matter? Two simple analogies are introduced below to help answer these questions.

* * *

Bicycles made their first appearance on park pathways in 1817 and were called "walking machines" and "hobby horses." Then, Karl Benz, who invented the gasoline engine in Germany, manufactured the first practical automobile in 1885. Twenty-three years later, Henry Ford began producing the *Model T Ford* in Detroit in 1908. Initially automobiles were built for convenient transportation from one place to another. They were a means of conveyance with many features a horse, wagon, or bicycle could not provide. In time, due to their availability to the general public, the choice of a family automobile went beyond convenience. Comfort became important, then economy, then style, and then luxury. A preference for a certain kind of automobile became normal.

"I'd really like to have a two-door coupe with a rumble seat in back."

The contrary to the preference also became common. "I would never drive or ride in a foreign-made automobile."

Disdainful comments toward a particular automobile began to verge on prejudice. "That model of car is a piece of junk and ought to be scrapped and banned from the roads!"

The attitudes our culture holds towards death, a vehicle that conveys us from life, is similar to the views about automobiles. When any person thinks of his or her own death, it is natural to have a preferred method. "I'd really like to just go to sleep and never wake up." It is also natural to think of different unwanted ways to die. "I would never want to die slowly in a car crash." Having a favorable or unfavorable opinion of a form of death reflects a preference and is a subtle type of bias.

The disdainful judgments against suicide as a way of dying are obvious in the remarks people make when learning about a self-inflicted death. This hurtful kind of prejudice can be directed at both the decedent and the survivors.

The biases against suicide are just as likely to be experienced and expressed among the decedent's family members as they are among strangers. When a suicide occurs within an intimate relationship, the survivor must come face-to-face with his own biases. How the survivor deals with his prejudices and feelings regarding suicide will greatly influence the course of his bereavement.

* * *

A young man who went to war gives us an example of how the absence of judgment would be recognized.

James Lewis Day enlisted in the Marine Corps at age 17, in the midst of the Second World War. Two years later, he was on the Island of Okinawa during one of the longest and bloodiest battles of the Pacific War. In May 1945, the Marines were fighting to drive the enemy defenders out of their fortified positions and off Sugar Loaf Hill. In the effort, two Marine regiments had been decimated. Besides the dead and wounded, some Marines had turned back from the assaults, retreating down the hill. Others had cradled in crater holes, unable to move an inch further up Sugar Loaf. Every now and then, a Marine had just stood up or had charged, unable to take any more punishment, and took a bullet or piece of shrapnel to end it.

On May 14th, in the middle of the battle, Corporal Day organized his squad and the remnants of another one and led them up the hill beyond the Marine front line into a heavy volume of artillery, mortars, grenades, and machine-gun fire. Within minutes of their advance from below, half of his men were dead. He did not freeze or withdraw and remained at the lead. When they reached a pivotal position on the hill, Corporal Day put his remaining men in fortified positions. Enemy soldiers charged time after time from their own entrenched positions. And, time after time, Corporal Day fought them back and, ignoring the intense enemy fire directed at him, carried wounded Marines to safety.

The fighting went on for three days, during which he sustained painful fragmentation wounds and white phosphorous burns. The final enemy attack came on the night of May 16 into the morning of the 17th. When the Marine line was finally able to advance to the top of Sugar Loaf Hill, Corporal Day and another wounded Marine were the only two survivors of his squad. For his actions, he earned a Medal of Honor, the highest award for valor our nation gives to its citizens.

From the crest of that hill, Jim Day did not consider himself anymore brave than any other Marine who had started up the hill. He was grateful to have survived the battle, attributing that reality to something far beyond his own courage. He did not expect tributes or medals. Nor did he judge or criticize those who had stopped, had cradled themselves in a crater, had turned back, or had deliberately stood up to take a fatal bullet. He understood and felt a deep and lasting bond with all of them.

Individuals fighting daily with depression or adverse circumstances or chronic pain of any kind each have their own Sugar Loaf Hill to climb. Naturally, times come when they feel impelled to go no further, to lie down and cradle themselves in a fortified position, or to go back down where it was once safe. Some are fortunate enough to have someone carry them until their hurts and wounds are relieved, and they can return to the climb. It is also natural that, when their minds and nervous systems can take no more of life's batterings, they want it all to end. The individuals who reach that moment deserve recognition for bravely starting out and going as far as they could, rather than the judgments of those able to advance further up the hill. Jim Day would tell us as much.

* * *

One result of judgments against self-inflicted death is that death has been categorized into types. In our society, for example, there is normal death and there is suicide. Normal death is comprised of all forms of death that are not suicidal. In this context, even homicide is viewed as normal. Although death is a normal, inevitable feature of being human, suicidal death is believed to be outside the range of normalcy. Since suicide is not normal, it is considered abnormal. As Wayne Weiten stated, "Our culture views suicide as an abnormal act to be prevented whenever possible, while some cultures consider suicide to be an acceptable and even courageous act under certain circumstances." [24]

The separation of death into normal and abnormal seems to be based on the intentions of the decedent. The common thread connecting all normal deaths is that the decedent had no apparent intention to die. Suicide is abnormal because the decedent apparently decided to die, intended to die, and engineered the death.

This categorization of death into normal and abnormal is based on arbitrary cultural attitudes. This point is developed further in the last chapters of this book. It is important here only to suggest that the division of types of death into normal and abnormal results in certain consequences for the suicide survivor. It makes suicide bereavement different.

There Seems So Little To Say After A Suicide

A third factor making suicide bereavement different from other grief experiences derives from the cultural biases against suicide.

When a person experiences the death of someone close to him, our society provides an outlet for grief by extending normal and established patterns of support to him. These social supports include acknowledgement of the death, funeral services, religious rites and ceremonies, comforting help and support, condolences, well wishes, encouragement, and acceptance of the survivor's grief reactions.

Most of us take these patterns of support for granted because they seem to occur automatically and naturally within the community. When we experience a death, we believe that there will be a supportive social response that is initiated without effort on the survivor's part. Again, we believe in and expect such social response. It is automatic.

Survivors of a suicide are more likely than others to discover that these social responses to death are not so automatic. In fact, these so-called "automatic" social responses might be denied to them. Although our society has an established ritual structure that permits acceptance for every other type of death, it does not for a suicidal death.

The funeral services and religious rites following a suicide are often obviously different. Comforting support for the survivor is often lacking or inadequate. Appropriate condolences seem nonexistent. The death is often denied or unacknowledged by others, so drastically in some instances, that it is as if the decedent had never existed. Finally, the survivor's reactions to the death are less fully understood and less easily accepted.

Regarding the attempt to extend condolences to anyone in grief, admittedly, comforters and survivors find themselves in a quandary. Our contemporary culture has generally conditioned us to not discuss death. So, when a family member, friend, or coworker experiences the death of a loved one, it is hard to find comforting and soothing words to say to them. Additionally, people can be uncomfortable with silence and crying, even though empathetic silence can be the best comfort to provide to someone who is crying. In such situations, many individuals rely on clichés and hollow reassurances.

Samuel Wallace found this to be a consistent experience among the survivors he interviewed. "They also realized that their friends did not know what to do or say either. Some friends avoided the subject, while others pretended that nothing had happened." [25]

Suicide survivors know all too well that others do not know what condolences and comments can be comforting and what comments bring a stabbing ache, no matter the good intentions in speaking them. They also know they find it challenging themselves to say something meaningful about the self-inflicted death.

* * *

"I remember the day I found out that my father died. Lots of people came but only one would talk to me about it."

Michael, 10-years-old [26]

> "Almost everyone I know did not want to talk to me about the suicide. I suppose they thought it was too painful to bring it up to me. Maybe it was a reminder to them that death can come so quickly. I don't know. I just know that the silences stabbed me at my heart."

A Survivor

* * *

These facts are so socially well recognized that, from time to time, articles about *Things Not to Say to Someone Who is Grieving* will appear in magazines like *Woman's Day* and *Psychology Today*. Old and new books on this subject are also available: for example, *Call Me If You Need Anything and Other Things Not to Say* by Cathy Peterson. [27] The lists of inappropriate condolences consistently include such comments as:

"Everything happens for a reason."
"He's in a better place now."
"At least she's not suffering anymore."

"I'm sure you did all you could."
"Let me know if you need anything."
"Give me a call if you need to talk."
"I know exactly how you feel."
"Time heals all wounds."
"God never gives you more than you can handle."

Careful consideration of each of these should make it clear why a suicide survivor, more than others, might find them offensive. Even the current trend for saying, "I'm sorry for your loss" to a survivor can spark an irritable and cursory response. "Why are *you* sorry? You didn't do anything."

Is Suicide Bereavement Unique?

Its unexpected nature, the biases against it, and the lack of supportive traditions following it have frequently led researchers to conclude that suicide survivors suffer a grief process that is very different from "normal" grieving. Some researchers maintain that suicide survivorship is actually unique in its pattern, expression, and resolution.

Suicide bereavement is unlikely to be truly unique in a general sense. Suggesting that there is suicide bereavement and then there are all other bereavements might lead to inaccurate perceptions of the suicide grief process. The misunderstandings about suicide itself already adversely impact the survivors, and more misconceptions regarding the grief they experience can ultimately only add to the survivor's confusion.

Suicide bereavement is not a singular and unique response to a self-inflicted death. By far, it is more similar to other forms of bereavement than it is different or unique. When the focus of bereavement is so much on the fact that the death was a suicide, however, the survivor often misses that the bereavement experience is predominantly the grief of loss of a loved one. The work of separation is impeded. Additionally, internal conflicts about how any death occurred always create obstructions to the resolution and recovery from the death.

As John Hewett portrayed, suicide bereavement is an accumulation of distinct types of reactions. These reactions, for the most part, resemble those experienced in other forms of grief. [28] Specifically, suicide bereavement is comprised primarily of at least four different types of grief reactions. These are:

1) *common or "normal" grief reactions* that are present in most experiences of grief;

2) *unexpected death reactions* that result from the lack of preparation for death, regardless of its cause;

3) *other-than-natural death reactions* that are experienced when a death results from other than natural causes; and,

4) *suicidal death reactions* that are more likely to be experienced in the event of self-inflicted death than in any other form of survivorship.

The next four chapters introduce the various types of reactions suicide survivors frequently report to describe their grief experiences. The individual reactions included within these descriptions are not complete or exhaustive in detailing suicide bereavement, and survivors might experience other reactions that are not outlined in the following descriptions. The grief reactions included in the following chapters are those that appear to be most frequent among suicide's survivors.

five

It's The Same, But Different

"A person's death is not only an ending; it is also a beginning for the survivors."
Edwin S. Shneidman [29]

Suicide, regardless of the social perceptions of its nature, is primarily the loss of a significant person from the life of the survivor, and the death brings a grief experience similar to that suffered by all other survivors. This means grief following suicide will primarily be comprised of grief reactions common to all forms of grief, whether the cause of death was natural, accident, homicide, or suicide.

This chapter describes the most common, or normal, grief reactions frequently reported by suicide survivors. For ease of presentation, these common, general reactions are divided into initial, primary, and later grief reactions.

Initial Grief Reactions

The initial reactions of survivors experiencing the death of a loved one mark the beginning of the grieving process. In the experience of suicide, the initial reactions of the survivors are, with little exception, the same reactions experienced after other types of death. These initial reactions include shock, disbelief, and severe sorrow.

SHOCK

The most consistent of the initial emotional reactions experienced by survivors upon learning of a suicide are primarily shock reactions. These reactions, sometimes described as psychic numbing, are similar to the shock experiences of trauma victims. Shock reactions are most evident among survivors unfortunate enough to discover the body of the decedent.

One indication of shock is feeling cold or an inability to feel warmth. Although this might be a generalized, vague sensation, the feeling of cold might be especially apparent in the hands and feet. A sensation of being or feeling numb is also common.

* * *

> "Even now I can't remember it. I just stood there. My daughter told me later that the officer said to me, 'Did you hear me? Why are you smiling?'"

* * *

A survivor in the initial phase of grief often appears to be in a dazed and preoccupied mental condition. She might perform tasks and go through motions with little awareness of her actions and afterwards might have poor memory of events.

"I can't think straight." The survivor commonly experiences a state of confusion initially. She might become easily disoriented as to the date, day, and time. She might also find it difficult to recognize where she is at, or remember a task she has set out to do. Ironically, during this mentally foggy period there can also be crystallization of certain events or feelings. These the survivor will vividly recall long after the bereavement. For example, the survivor might not be able to forget a friend's facial expression, the scent of someone's perfume, or a remark overheard in passing. Though the survivor might not recall greeting some people who offered condolences, she might remain painfully and acutely aware that others did not extend their sympathies or attend memorial and funeral services.

The experience of shock usually includes a general feeling of emptiness, generally described by survivors as a feeling of emptiness in the stomach. Although their nerves are actually open, raw, and terribly vulnerable, many survivors initially sense an absence of feeling.

In other forms of death, shock reactions usually last only a few days, dissipating into other normal grief reactions. However, in suicide the shock reaction can be extended, lasting in part as long as weeks after the funeral. This might be especially true for survivors who have discovered the body of the deceased.

DISBELIEF

Among all survivors, there is a strong tendency to resist accepting the reality that death has occurred. Such denial of death is expressed in various ways.

Denial, or disbelief, is evident in many of the survivor's remarks. Examples include exclamations like: "No!", "This isn't happening," or "It can't be true." The survivor might argue emotionally with the person who brings news of the death. Demands to see the body as proof of the death are also common. Some survivors deny death so strongly that, when viewing or identifying the decedent's body, they will insist it is not the decedent.

Disbelief takes other, more subtle forms. For example, a survivor might continue to daily anticipate the decedent's return home. She might cling stubbornly to habits and routines they had shared or look for the deceased in places they had been together. The survivor might also imagine or make up evidence to convince herself that the deceased is still alive.

Although disbelief is a common experience in all deaths, it takes an odd twist in suicide. Survivors of suicidal death tend also to deny the cause of death, that is, they deny that death occurred due to a suicidal method. Discounting both the fact that death has occurred and the cause of the death is an additional burden normally not experienced by other survivors. Since denial of the cause of death is almost absolutely unique to suicide, it is discussed in greater detail in Chapter Eight.

In other forms of death, shreds of disbelief typically endure for periods of several days or weeks. Seldom are the realities of the death avoided as the months right after the death go by. In the event of suicide, however, disbelief or denial, tend to last longer. Denial is most prominent in the first few weeks following the suicide, but has also been evident in some cases as long as months or years after the death.

SEVERE SORROW

The reactions of shock and disbelief gradually give way to intense feelings of sadness. These feelings of severe sorrow are not to be confused with depression. This sorrow is comprised of the grief reactions most widely expected of the survivor and most easily accepted by others.

Survivors experience severe sorrow in many obvious ways. They encounter sensations of physical distress that occur periodically and in waves lasting from minutes up to an hour at a time. They commonly cry, weep, or wail for extended periods. Some survivors frequently feel an obvious need to sigh deeply. Some also experience sensations like tightness of the throat, difficulty in catching one's breath, shortness of breath, and an emptiness of the abdomen.

A general physical lethargy often overtakes the survivor. Physical activity of any intensity can become difficult. Short walks, climbing stairs, carrying objects, exercising, even eating can become impossible endeavors. Disturbed sleep, loss of appetite, muscular pains, and general irritability might also be experienced.

Survivors usually try to suppress the intense feelings of sorrow. Most individuals are frightened both by the strength of these feelings and by the sensation of emotions run amuck. However, intense feelings of sorrow can be repressed only for short periods. Eventually, they well up and break through to the surface. When that happens, their renewed intensity can be both devastating and overwhelming.

* * *

> "I would just start crying. I couldn't stop, and
> I thought it was never going to end."
>
> A Survivor

* * *

The reaction of severe sorrow is often accompanied by other significant changes in the observable behavior of the bereaved survivor. Intense sorrow can generate increased and troubling anxiety. To combat such anxiety, a survivor might turn to increased use of alcohol, prescription medications, or cigarettes. This can then complicate already disturbed patterns of sleep, appetite, and mood.

In most cases of bereavement, the intensity of the sorrow reaction generally begins to subside after the first months following the death, gradually and slowly decreasing in severity thereafter. This is also true among suicide survivors, although remnants of severe sorrow can be present years after the death.

The Initial Reactions Are Grief's Buffer

Initial grief reactions are essentially the same after all types of death. After suicide, however, they seem to endure a little longer than in other forms of bereavement. Thus, suicide survivors might take longer to navigate the initial course of grieving and lag behind on the road to recovery. This fact has led many researchers to differentiate suicide bereavement from other forms of grief. In the words of Samuel Wallace, suicide "produces the most intense grieving of any type of death. Whether it is labeled complicated, acute, or any other term, its intensity is searing to the survivor." [30]

In most bereavements, the initial grief reactions of shock, disbelief, and severe sorrow are often accompanied by other reactions such as relief, anger, hostility, panic attacks, a sense of abandonment, and restlessness. These reactions intrude erratically and do not occur as consistently as shock, disbelief, and severe sorrow in the early period of grief. They are a prelude to the significant and longer lasting reactions that grief embodies. The initial reactions buffer the survivor from the wide array of other grief reactions that are coming.

When shock and disbelief begin to subside, and before the recovery process has begun, the survivor comes face-to-face with many emotions. The emotions that follow the initial reactions to death are called "primary grief reactions" in this book.

Calling this complex of troubling emotions and experiences *primary reactions* might be a little misleading. These reactions can be present in the immediate aftermath of death in most bereavements. They might also exist later in the bereavement when recovery has progressed significantly. However, these reactions are typically more predominant only after shock, disbelief, and severe sorrow dissipate and usually before recovery begins. Therefore, they are referred to here as the primary grief reactions.

Two facts are important regarding the primary grief reactions. First of all, they are always intense and are rooted deep in the psyche (meaning the human mind, consciousness, or spirit) of the individual. Therefore, the expression of grief reactions typically involves the whole person. The reactions are not easily, nor without consequence, repressed, blunted, inhibited, nor circumvented. Second, there are few times in any survivor's life when so many different and terribly strong emotions threaten to burst into consciousness at the same time.

Since grief is typically an infrequent experience, its impact is hard to imagine and nearly impossible to passively anticipate. For this single reason, most individuals are not emotionally or psychologically prepared for their encounter with grief.

If the primary grief reactions arose as an immediate consequence to someone's death, the survivor would likely be quickly overcome by their combined intensities. The expected result might well be a breakdown or disintegration of the person on some level, whether emotional, physical, psychological, spiritual, or intellectual. However, because a basic motivation to survive exists in all individuals, the human psyche intervenes to protect a survivor from the full impact of another's death.

The psyche protects the person by initiating the shock reaction. Instead of allowing the survivor to be instantly flooded with powerful and frightful grief emotions, shock blunts the response to the intense feelings, doing so to the extent that the survivor is only vaguely aware of the impact of these sensations. Thus, shock gives the survivor time to prepare for the onslaught of the surfacing emotions and does not usually subside until the person is somewhat ready to deal with them.

Not only does the shock reaction initially blunt and buffer the emotions, it also functions in another manner. As shock wears off, it filters the emotions that arise. This means the emotions do not flood upon the survivor all at once, or all at the same time. The survivor usually encounters each emotion in waves, a little bit at a time.

This, in part, explains why the grief reactions often endure longer for survivors of suicide than for other survivors. The greater number and increased intensity of the reactions they experience means the reactions will take longer both to surface and to be resolved by the survivor.

Primary Grief Reactions

Any and all reactions to death are fully human and natural. They are all perfectly normal, regardless of how common or rare they might be. If a human experiences the reaction, it must be a normal human reaction. The primary grief reactions essentially are normal expressions of emotions that are consequences to a loss.

Suicide survivors do not necessarily experience all of the primary reactions described below. Nor do they experience them in any particular order. Some of these reactions occur consistently among suicide survivors, others are less common. The primary grief reactions frequently encountered by survivors of suicidal death are the focus here.

Remembering that grief is an ongoing process, and not a set of reactions occurring in a given sequence or developing in a fixed pattern of stages, many of the reactions described below as primary reactions are present immediately in the experience of grief. They are not predominant initially, however, because of the function of shock. Other of these reactions emerge over time as the initial grief reactions subside.

The intensity of these emotional reactions is directly related to the depth and strength of the relationship that had been established with the deceased. Consequently, family members suffer a grief more intense than that suffered by friends, who in turn experience grief that is more painful than that suffered by casual acquaintances.

It is critical to the health of the survivor that each and every one of the grief emotions has ample expression. The survivor is likely to find these emotions somehow frightening, but their repression results in further complication of the grief process and later problems of adjustment. In other words, if the survivor places limits on how much grief she will deal with consciously, limits will also be imposed upon the level of recovery and readjustment to life she will achieve.

* * *

> "I turned so sensitive and needy. I'd break down
> if I couldn't remember where I put things, and
> friends were calling me all the time to remind me
> where I was supposed to be. It was awful."
>
> A Survivor

* * *

After shock, disbelief, and severe sorrow weaken their hold on the survivor, among the reactions that commonly surface are preoccupation with the deceased, guilt, anger, depression, loneliness, flight into activity, need to talk, relief, and feeling deserted.

PREOCCUPATION WITH THE DECEASED

Death does not mean that the deceased just suddenly disappears and goes away forever from the life of the survivor. Even after the funeral services and burial, the survivor must deal with the vivid presence of the deceased in her daily life, a presence that goes beyond the mere preoccupation with thoughts and memories of the deceased.

There is a strong instinct within the survivor to at least hold on to him for as long as possible, if not regain the lost person entirely. This occurs both consciously and unconsciously. For one thing, memories are very often extremely clear visualizations. The survivor can conjure up in her mind the decedent's face, body, voice, mannerisms, and characteristics no less vividly than if the deceased could physically materialize before her.

The survivor's reflections upon events experienced with the decedent might also take on a clarity that they did not have previously. Past, incidental details are brought to light, as if they had recently happened.

The survivor's dreams of the decedent, rarely about the death itself, can be experienced as real. Dreams are more likely of happier past events or of the often-wished-for return of the deceased. Upon awakening from sleep, the survivor can be disturbed by the realization that the brief joy of reunion with the decedent was a dream, and then yearn to go back into the cherished dream.

It is not unusual for a survivor to search for the deceased, trying to feel his presence nearby or in familiar places. She might maintain familiar routines, like continuing to set an extra place at the supper table, or laying out the decedent's clothes in the morning. In nearly every case of bereavement, the survivor continues to talk to the decedent as if he can still hear and reply. Later, this might take the form of a silent prayer or a brief thought. This tendency seems never to fully go away.

Some survivors feel strong urges to go to the same places the deceased frequented. On occasion, she might he startled by the sensation of briefly catching a glimpse of the decedent in a crowd. The survivor might even call out to him, expecting a response.

Often, the survivor believes the decedent will somehow make contact and let the survivor know he is nearby. Many survivors report the actual appearance of the decedent. In these extreme cases, survivors might say the decedent's apparition passively observed her, carried a message, performed a task, or engaged in conversation. Survivor's who have this experience describe an encounter so real they are unable to accurately discern whether it happened in reality or in their imagination.

Most survivors spend a great deal of time thinking about the last days of the deceased. Among those who witnessed the progression of a terminal illness, it is common to painfully recall how the deceased might have suffered or how peacefully he died. Great importance is placed upon whether or not the survivor was actually present at the death.

Ruminations of suicide survivors tend especially to focus on the moment of death. More so than in other deaths, the images of self-inflicted death seem to capture the survivor's rapt attention. These images, though conjured up less frequently as time passes, are likely to retain the vividness of a photograph even years after the death.

GUILT

Guilt is a predominant and normal part of any grief and is experienced in several forms. Unless the relationship between the survivor and decedent was somehow seriously disturbed or dysfunctional, these forms of guilt are typically transient and not difficult to resolve as the grief progresses.

Following a death, guilt usually develops regarding events that occurred during the life of the relationship. The survivor often regrets things said or done in anger. She might have a sense of having not done enough to make the decedent's life pleasant. Very often, the survivor berates herself for negligence toward the decedent's needs and wishes. The survivor can exaggerate even minor omissions until they take unrealistic proportions.

* * *

"She liked it when I wrote a little "lovey" in her day planner. I knew that. You'd think I could have done it more often."

A Survivor

* * *

Sometimes, grieving persons experience a form of "survivor guilt." This involves a perception that the decedent's death was somehow unfair and that, in some ways, it might have been better for the survivor to have been the one to die.

Finally, guilt can also be a counter-reaction to other natural grief feelings. For instance, feeling anger, shame or relief in regard to the decedent's death can seem inappropriate or wrong to the survivor and triggers more guilt.

Suicide survivors experience much the same guilt as other survivors. They review past interactions with the deceased and sense guilt for acts or omissions that might in some way have disturbed the decedent's peace of mind. They sometimes think they should have died in place of the decedent, and they feel guilt over their anger, shame, or relief.

Guilt following suicide is compounded if the survivor believes that she shares in the responsibility for the death or that she contributed to it in a significant way. Suicide survivors commonly analyze the events immediately preceding the death, over and over again, to determine the degree of blame they share with the decedent for the suicide.

The survivor frequently thinks she could have, or should have, done something to prevent the suicide. Some even think that if it were not for the survivor, the deceased would not have completed suicide. Consequently, the survivor might believe the death is her fault.

Survivors who experience accidents, homicides, and surprise illnesses also struggle to resolve this guilt of culpability. Yet, for these other survivors of sudden, unexpected death the sense that there might have been more they could have done to prevent the death is typically not as strong as it is for the suicide survivor. The facts surrounding the death can usually reassure them that they were not responsible for it.

Alfred Alvarez believes that "suicide is distasteful to the survivors if for no other reason than that it so effortlessly promotes guilt." [31] While guilt is a common grief reaction in most other bereavements, it is a predominant reaction in suicide survivorship.

Several factors potentially complicate the suicide survivor's guilt. First of all, suicide usually involves at least two people who were engaged in a close, intimate relationship. The deceased has made a choice to end his life, and in a very significant way has rejected the support of the survivor. The implication to the survivor is that she did not make life pleasant enough or meaningful enough or some other "mysterious enough" to make the decedent want to stay alive.

Some survivors perceive the suicide as revenge, a retribution given by the decedent for some critical act or omission. In many cases, this might be an accurate assessment of the decedent's intentions. According to Ronald W. Maris, revenge suicides are more prevalent than is usually believed. [32] In other words, many individuals take their own lives as a way to get even with someone. Apparently, this element of revenge is more likely among younger suicides, high alcohol users, and persons making more than one suicide attempt. The implication of revenge makes it very difficult, if not impossible, for the survivor to exclude her interactions with the decedent from factors that contributed to the suicide.

Another factor compounding the guilt and contributing to a perception of shared responsibility and fault in the death is a sensation that the survivor should have known the suicide was going to happen. Ronald Maris suggests that many survivors were aware on some level of the decedent's pre-suicidal symptoms or clues, but were either unable or unwilling to intervene in time to stop the suicide. That most, but certainly not all, suicidal persons give hints, clues, and warnings of their intentions to end their own lives has become an accepted fact. Edwin Shneidman estimated that as many as 80% of those who complete suicide gave clear and definite warnings of their suicidal intentions. [33]

The existence or hints of clues and warnings not heeded presents a dilemma for the suicide survivor. Only after the suicide does the survivor recall the obvious and subtle ways the decedent was broadcasting his plans to die. As the survivor unearths pre-suicidal warning signs, it becomes increasingly more difficult to detach from responsibility and culpability in the death. The survivor naturally concludes that, if she had paid attention to the decedent's threatened intentions, she would have been able to prevent the suicide.

There are cases of surprise or "blitz" suicides in which the death seems to come out of nowhere and is not preceded by obvious clues or warnings. Even following these, a survivor will seem bent on expending a great deal of effort reflecting upon the past, searching for subtle hints of the decedent's suicidal intentions. Quite often the survivor places undue significance upon trivial or minor events that were totally unrelated to the eventual death.

Whether clues are discovered or not, the consequences remain the same. The survivor will sense that warnings were made, that she should have understood their significance, and that she should have prevented the suicide.

Acknowledging that pre-suicidal warnings existed is important for the survivor, if in fact they did. However, it is equally important to understand that, if the decedent did give clues and warnings, it does not mean that the survivor was able, at the time and in the context of their close relationship, to pick up on them or perceive them for what they were. Survivors are often the last to see warnings or clues, because they cared so deeply about the decedent they could not recognize the depth of his pain.

Additionally, even if the survivor received obvious and clear warnings, there is a strong human tendency to believe that suicide will not really be completed. As Gerald Ginsburg observed, it is not that persons close to the suicidal individual are blind to his clues, it is simply that they interpret them improperly. [34] Most people do not believe that a person who hints or declares that he intends to end his own life will actually do so. This implies that people are likely to ignore or disregard threats mainly because they do not believe them. Survivors who had experienced a decedent's previous suicide attempts often describe their inability to believe that the suicide would follow the "clues" and warnings, even when they had been made anxious by recognizing them.

The intensity and complexity of the guilt following a suicide contribute significantly to the bereavement. Although suicide survivors might not resolve the issue of guilt quickly or completely, most appear to manage and work through the guilt successfully, not allowing it to hamper their recovery any more than do other survivors.

ANGER

An individual experiencing grief generally senses feelings of irritability and bitterness at one time or another. A survivor might react with impatience, irritability, or anger toward various people during the grieving process.

Such feelings are frequently part of a pervasive anger that boils within the survivor and quite often bubbles to the surface. Anger of this kind can result in aggressive or irrational behavior that is usually uncharacteristic of the survivor. Although the survivor might have some awareness of an incessant anger toward the decedent or the death, the anger is seldom expressed as outright rage at the decedent for having left the survivor behind.

Anger is a normal result of any significant loss. Death usually means that an important source of satisfaction and gratification has been lost to the survivor. It often means the loss of a source of love, support, companionship, or pleasure. On some psychological level, the survivor might believe that the decedent has stolen these satisfactions away by dying, and outbursts of anger might unconsciously become associated with thoughts of him.

* * *

"I was blind with rage for what he had done!
How dare him to do this to me!"

A Survivor

* * *

Survivors frequently experience the nagging suspicion that they have been deserted by the decedent. Similar to a child's experience of separation anxiety, common responses to being left behind are initially anger outbursts and temper tantrums.

Anger during bereavement is more than a response to loss. It also serves a definite function in the process of grieving, for it is significantly instrumental in facilitating the survivor's struggles to successfully separate emotionally from the deceased and to rebuild a life in which he is a missing part.

As is true in other grief reactions, there is a twist in the anger reaction of a suicide survivor. The heightened sense of guilt and responsibility after a suicide makes it terribly painful for the survivor to accept that such anger exists and to direct the anger toward the decedent. Denial of anger toward its obvious and rightful object usually results in its expression, with considerable force, upon others.

Samuel Wallace found that suicide survivors often cast irrational blame upon those around them, possibly to forestall the acknowledgement that the decedent made a choice to complete suicide.[35] They commonly bellow against officials and institutions rather than directing their anger toward the decedent. Searching for scapegoats, they might target their rage against doctors, policemen, coroners, insurance investigators, morticians, and hospital personnel. Other such innocents like store clerks, garage mechanics, or deliverymen can be the targets of the survivor's rage. Although it is helpful to vent anger rather than keep it inside, the unfortunate consequence of redirecting grief anger is that it subverts anger's normal function of aiding in the separation from the deceased.

The hesitation to express anger appropriately toward the decedent and the death creates further problems. If the survivor directs the anger toward those who would normally want to talk about the suicide, the survivor will likely be alienated from the needed support of others.

Additionally, if the survivor continues to deny the presence of anger, or directs the anger at inappropriate targets, working through the grief becomes more difficult. In such circumstances, the normal functions of anger to bring the hurt to light and to help the emotional separation from the deceased are blocked. Holding onto the anger also preserves the bond with the decedent and allows the survivor to hold on to him for a longer time.

DEPRESSION

Grieving is an internal experience, profoundly subjective and in many ways individualistic. Comprehending the various emotions that emerge during bereavement is often difficult for people, even for those who have previously been through a grief. It is understandable, then, for the survivor and those around her to be confused about what exactly is happening to her.

The survivor experiences various reactions comprising the process of grieving after a death, and grief is unquestionably a sorrowful time. Deep sadness is merely a part of grief, not in and of itself, the total composition of the grief experience.

One common misinterpretation of the grief experience equates sorrow with depression. Sorrow is not depression, especially in bereavement. After any loss, it would be far more appropriate to say the survivor is grieving, rather than to say she is depressed. However, experiencing the death of a loved one is an event that can bring on either a biological or situational depression.

Genuine depression is a reaction that develops over a period of time. It does not just drop upon the survivor full blown at the outset of grieving. A depression that develops during grieving might be a consequence or offshoot of several other reactions common to grief. This is because many reactions considered to be symptoms of depression are also inherent to the grief process. These reactions include changes in sleeping patterns and in appetite, dampened emotional reaction, loss of sexual drive, loss of interest in once valued pursuits, suicidal thoughts, anger, and guilt. The combined effects of these normal grief reactions can accumulate and coagulate resulting in the development of the depression condition.

Several theories regarding the source of depression have been formulated. One is especially relevant to the explanation of the grief process. This theory maintains that depression can result from a significant loss. According to the significant loss theory, anything with close association to a person acquires importance. This thing can be anything seemingly as trivial as a doll, rock collection, book, or pet, or as major as a person, child, relationship, job, house, or town. Eventually, the person actually internalizes the important thing. In other words, the important thing becomes part of the person.

Once an object, possession, or other person has been internalized, it not only feels like a part of the involved person, it also becomes an attachment to the person. This bond feels much like any other ownership. When one person becomes an internalized part of another, loss of that person is painful to the other, because the loss is felt, at least in part, as a loss of self.

The ensuing reaction after loss of an important person is similar to what happens when infants and young children experience separation from a parent. A fear that the parent will not return is normal. This "separation anxiety" is characterized by vigorous outbursts of angry crying. If the instinctive reaction brings the parent back to the child and is repeated often enough, the child learns that having angry outbursts is effective in bringing back a lost object, that is, the parent. The child is relieved of their fear.

This is true only if the parent returns to the child. If the child's angry protest at the loss does not bring the separated parent back, the angry protest will eventually subside. Gradually, after occasional tantrums, the child will slip into a numbed state similar to sorrow.

During bereavement, when the initial grief reactions of shock and denial have begun to subside, the death of a significant person is eventually understood to be a permanent separation. At this point, the survivor comprehends that the deceased is physically irretrievable. Naturally, she then experiences the pain of losing someone who was a part of her self. The survivor also feels tremendous anger at experiencing the loss, or more appropriately, the snatching away of something that was hers.

As explained above in the section about anger, individuals grieving do not always express the understandable rage that boils within them. According to the significant loss theory, the survivor therefore ends up turning this anger inward. Unable to express the anger openly, the survivor takes it out on herself. She becomes her own target. The survivor becomes depressed. In this view, depression is anger turned inward against oneself.

Once depression has developed, the survivor experiences many symptoms. The most typical is a sense of being sad or unhappy and an inability to overcome it. She might feel hopeless, terribly discouraged about the future, and pessimistic about life. The survivor might be especially critical of herself, finding fault and blame for her actions. She might also he disappointed or disgusted with herself or feel like a failure in life.

Depression commonly includes a sense of guilt or unworthiness and an impression that one is being, or should be, punished. There might be a feeling of being ugly, repulsive, or unattractive in appearance. A pervasive sense of being annoyed or irritated, uncontrollable fits of crying or loss of all emotion, an oppressive dissatisfaction or loss of interest in all things, and an inability to concentrate or make decisions are all typical reactions.

Physical and mental fatigue often build to the point that the survivor finds it difficult to get out of bed or finds it impossible to accomplish any work. There might be increased sleep, an inability to sleep, or different patterns of disturbed sleep.

Depressed individuals often become more aware and concerned about their physical health, experiencing problems of stomach and headaches, various body pains, constipation and diarrhea. They might also experience a loss or increase of appetite and a weight loss or gain. Loss of sexual drive and interest is common.

Finally, depressed people can experience a loss of will to live or an active interest in dying. They are often prone to accidents and suicide. Fortunately, most people who develop severe depression lack the energy and ability to plan in the extreme measure that suicide requires. Typically, extreme depression is so debilitating that the person is unable to deliberately take his/her own life through a single act of suicide. The risk of suicide actually increases when the depression begins to lift, and more energy is available.

The presence of any one of these symptoms just described does not necessarily indicate that depression has developed during grief. Clinically, depression is diagnosed by measuring the presence of a number of these symptoms. In most cases when depression is diagnosed, a cluster of symptoms is present.

Differentiating between what is called reactive, or acute, depression and endogenous (biological) depression is a helpful way to understand the emergence of depression as a grief reaction. Reactive depression is a response, or reaction, to an external event. A person becomes depressed as a result of something that has happened outside of herself—the external event that would generally and typically be viewed as "depressing."

It should be apparent that many common grief reactions are also common symptoms of depression. Therefore, it is not surprising that nearly all survivors experience some degree of depression. In most cases, grief depression is a form of reactive depression, meaning grief depression is merely a natural reaction to the death of a significant person.

Endogenous depression, on the other hand, is not precipitated by an outside event. Rather, the depression originates from within the person. Believed to be caused by chemical imbalances in the brain and central nervous system, clinicians typically regard endogenous depression to be more insidious, harder to understand, and more difficult to treat than reactive depression. More severe and longer lasting, endogenous depression usually requires professional intervention and drug therapy. Understandably, the additional acute depression activated by grief can be overwhelming for anyone already dealing with endogenous depression.

Depression is a minor reaction of short duration for some survivors. For others it can be severe and interminable. Any depression that becomes chronic, whether it is called grief, reactive, acute, or endogenous, is dangerous. Therefore, chronic and severe depression lasting longer than four consecutive weeks is a threat to the survivor's life and should be treated professionally.

Determining whether suicide survivors experience a more profound or severe depression than survivors of other forms of death is difficult. Depression is hard to quantify and it is a challenge to differentiate natural grief reactions from depressive symptoms. At this time, there is little research evidence to support even an intuitive inference suggesting that suicide bereavement includes a depressive reaction more intense or enduring than other bereavements.

LONELINESS

Bereaved survivors obviously experience a sense of being left alone after the death of someone they loved. Most relatives, friends, and comforters of the survivor make this common assumption—a primary motivation for them to keep in contact with the survivor, even if infrequently.

As time passes after the death, the survivor often hears comments like "I didn't want you to be lonely tonight," or "Why don't you come out with us so you won't have to be alone." Although some survivors are sensitive to such remarks and resent them as intrusions upon their solitude, most survivors tend to respond well to invitations for company and appreciate the offers.

Depending on the social circumstances of the survivor, loneliness usually dissipates significantly in the later stages of the grief process. This is true especially if other grief reactions have been resolved and recovery from the grief and reintegration into life are underway.

In some, but certainly not all cases, the loneliness of the suicide survivor follows a different course. Survivors often withdraw into themselves seeking explanations for the suicide. As bereavement continues, the survivor's loneliness can also deepen and intensify as a result of denial, guilt, anger, shame, blame, and depression.

Some survivors unintentionally push would-be comforters away because of the disturbing feelings they encounter after a suicide. In extreme cases they react with outraged hostility at the offer of company from others. Under such circumstances, comforters are unlikely to persist in their efforts to provide support to the survivor. This not only results from the hostility and strong emotions they encounter in their interactions with the survivor, but also from their own desires to avoid the suicidal nature of the death.

Alienation and isolation of a survivor will potentially increase feelings of loneliness, ensuring that the impact of feeling alone in the world will endure for longer periods of time than is normal following bereavement.

One other feature of grief within a family can amplify loneliness for individual survivors. Besides the loss of the decedent, a survivor might feel the loss of others who are buried in their own shock and bereavement. "Two things happened to me on January 11, 1992. I lost my brother to death, and lost my parents to grief." [36]

FLIGHT INTO ACTIVITY

Many survivors, no matter what the cause of death, seem to develop a pattern of restless busyness soon after the death. Typically, this reaction manifests itself within the first weeks of grieving. It is noticeable as busy work, as moving about in an agitated and purposeless manner, as an inability to sit still, as going about touching familiar things as if exploring them for something, or as a constant push to find something with which to occupy one's self.

There is an irony in this restlessness. As Erich Lindemann pointed out, all this activity is done with an apparent lack of zest or energy. [37] The survivor just goes through the motions. Even in the flurry of this activity, the survivor experiences a painful lack of capacity to initiate and maintain purposeful, organized patterns of effort. Although she might cling to the daily routine of habitual or prescribed activities, the survivor does so only with tremendous exertion, until she reaches a point of exhaustion.

* * *

> "It seems bizarre when I think of it. I was cleaning from dawn to past midnight, day after day, and the house always seemed more cluttered than when I started."
>
> A Survivor

* * *

The survivor's flight into activity serves a purpose. Keeping busy allows her to avoid, for periods of time, the many overwhelming and disturbing reactions inherent to grief. Sticking to established routines, the survivor unconsciously tries to minimize the significance of the loss. Initially in shock, the survivor hoped to convince herself that the loss did not occur. When the facts and reality of the death cannot be avoided, the survivor tries to prove to herself that the loss did not greatly change things.

Flight into activity is purposeful in another way. At a frightening time when the survivor's emotional life is disintegrating and her psychological stability might be deteriorating, activity is a frantic grasp to hold as much of herself together as possible. Thus, flight into activity can be both a form of denial of the importance of the loss and an attempt to regain control of a life that has suddenly been turned inside out.

One common consequence of flight into activity is physical exhaustion. Perhaps unable to sleep, the survivor keeps busy for extensive portions of the day and night. Eventually, when activity can no longer be sustained, the survivor collapses into inactivity and sleep. A cycle of activity and exhaustion temporarily develops. In most cases when this happens, the survivor regains a balance between activity and rest in a month or two.

A pattern of enduring, chronic hyperactivity is a potential consequence of flight into activity if it is not recognized as a grief reaction. The survivor might learn, consciously or unconsciously, that by compulsively finding things to do and filling time, she can avoid troublesome memories and thoughts. Once started, the survivor relentlessly pursues activity. Grieving is blocked and she never slows down.

Many suicide survivors do evidently develop patterns of activity that resemble hyperactivity, but it is hard to say whether flight into activity is more prevalent among suicide survivors than other survivors. The experience of hyperactivity might be an explanation for the suggestion by researchers that suicide survivors seem prone to stress-related heart conditions.

NEED TO TALK

The survivor's feelings toward the decedent do not die with the death, and working through the feelings that remain for the decedent becomes a major task of grieving. The survivor talking freely and openly about the decedent and the death facilitates this task.

The survivor really cannot talk enough about the decedent. In fact, it is healthy for her to talk and talk and talk until she can talk no more. Talking endlessly about the decedent might very well be the best therapy for grief. Doing so is usually expected early in the bereavement and readily accepted by those around her. Encouraging the survivor to talk about the decedent can actually be the greatest support provided. Comforters often have no more to do than to ask how she is doing and lend an understanding ear. There is little another can say to relieve the survivor's grief anyway.

Unfortunately, as grief continues, the survivor too often encounters people who are uncomfortable talking about the decedent and the death. The survivor inevitably senses this discomfort. Perhaps more sensitive to the other's feelings than the comforter is to hers, the survivor begins avoiding that about which she most clearly wishes to talk. In this way the need for talking is often prematurely obstructed. Subsequently, the survivor constrains herself to conversation more acceptable and comfortable to the "comforters."

"I can't even say his name." Something unusual and possibly embarrassing often happens to a survivor who cannot, for whatever reason, talk freely about the grief. Although generally appearing listless and lethargic, she might suddenly engage energetically in conversation about the deceased. The survivor can experience a great drive or pressure to talk about the decedent. Words come in a flurry and rush. The survivor's conversation appears to have been bottled up. Once uncorked, little can prevent it from gushing forth. Psychologists sometimes refer to this rush of conversation as "pressure of speech."

Aspects of suicidal death make it crucial for the survivor to talk about the decedent and the death. Certainly, the intensity of the emotional reactions to suicide and the need to explain the death dictate that the survivor will experience a heightened need to talk things through. However, the nature of suicidal death makes talking about the death more difficult than in other bereavements. As the survivor struggles to break through denial of the realities of the suicide and the urges to avoid various details surrounding the death, the grief work is slowed or stalled.

Generally, people find it difficult to be open about the kind of feelings predominant during suicide bereavement, like guilt, blame, anger, rejection, and shame. Instead of talking out these feelings with another, the suicide survivor withdraws and isolates herself, trying to deal with troubling emotions alone.

Finally, the likelihood that the survivor will reflect objectively on the life and death of the decedent decreases if she does not talk openly about them. Without shared objectivity, memories can take on powerful proportions and become distorted.

For suicide survivors, then, freely and openly discussing the death with others is especially important.

FEELING DESERTED

Nearly all survivors, at one time or another, feel the decedent has deserted them. This can simply be a feeling of being left alone, or left behind. It can also be a sensation of being forgotten by the deceased. A survivor finding life diminished, unsatisfactory, or overly burdened following the death often holds the decedent accountable for life's changed circumstances, as if a day will come when the decedent will have to make it up to the survivor for his unwelcome departure. These can be strong feelings for a survivor left with responsibilities once shared by the decedent. Any survivor who must continue to raise children, pay off bills, handle financial commitments, or manage a business without the support of the deceased is likely to feel deserted by him at some points.

* * *

> "You never said goodbye,
> You never told me why,
> You had to go,
> And leave me here alone."
>
> Lyla Jackson [38]

* * *

Some survivors manage feeling deserted with humor. They keep a tally of things they intend to tell the decedent when they are rejoined. They make oaths to chew the decedent out if they ever catch up with him. They draw the decedent's attention to their triumphs and trials as if he is watching. Other survivors, sadly, react to feeling deserted with bitterness, resentment, and blame. They continue to hold the decedent responsible for various misfortunes long after the death.

The realities of the death in most bereavements usually make it clear to the survivor that the deceased did not deliberately choose to leave her behind. The feeling of being deserted disappears with time. If it resurfaces later at anniversaries, birthdays, holidays, and special events, the sensation is fleeting and often handled openly with humor.

Among suicide survivors, feeling deserted is complicated by the nature of the death. If the survivor sees the death as the decedent's choice to die, it is harder not to take the suicide personally. Therefore, this reaction to suicide is usually more than a fleeting sensation of desertion. In fact, suicide survivors often face feelings of deliberate abandonment and rejection.

Abandonment and rejection are special grief reactions and are described in greater detail in Chapters Seven and Eight.

RELIEF

Survivors sometimes feel relieved when a death occurs, especially if the relationship with the decedent was in some way emotionally burdensome for the survivor. Although the death is painful, it also lifts the weight of the relationship from her.

This reaction is common when death follows a long illness, disability, or incapacitation, even if the condition was a mental illness. For one thing, the death might halt accruing financial difficulties these circumstances bring upon families. For another, when more and more of the survivor's time is spent in caretaking, there is less time for the activities that bring enjoyment and serve as a balance for life stresses. Relief is also apparent among survivors who had been involved in a dissatisfying relationship with the decedent: for example, relationships in which the decedent was alcoholic or abusive or had suffered from a personality disorder. In such cases, survivors had often already emotionally or physically separated from the decedent before the death occurred.

Experiencing relief can be problematic, because it arouses some guilt for the survivor. Feeling relief that someone has died seems calloused and inappropriate. On the other hand, relief dampens the intensity of other grief reactions and fosters completion of the grief work.

* * *

> "We had been to the emergency room so many times, taking out loans to pay the bills, picking him up at the bus depot, waiting for a call after midnight, listening to friends tell us we were just enabling the whole thing. Am I bad to feel a little bit relieved that the calls have stopped?"
>
> A Survivor

* * *

Suicide survivors do not appear to experience a sense of relief any more or less frequently than others. Survivors who experience a surprise suicide tend not to experience any sense of relief initially, unless the relationship with the decedent had somehow been an emotional burden. Survivors who had been manipulated with previous suicide threats or attempts are the ones most likely to report feeling relief after the death.

Later Grief Reactions

The grief reactions described so far are reactions suicide survivors share in common with all other survivors. They are also reactions that typically arise early in bereavement. The remaining reactions described in this chapter, ones usually outside a survivor's awareness until later in the bereavement, are also common reactions among all survivors. These reactions are unlikely to emerge early in the grief, because they ordinarily result from the cumulative effects of enduring grief. Additionally, they are typically overshadowed by the prominent early grief reactions and are unlikely to be acknowledged by the survivor until later.

Among the later recognized reactions are loss of self-worth, self-destructive behavior, physical illness, withdrawal and isolation, idealization, and loss of libido (sexual drive).

LOSS OF SELF-WORTH

This reaction to death is closely related to the concept of significant loss described in the development of depression. When we love someone, we form a bond with that person. Unconsciously, we internalize the person, who becomes a part of us. From a psychological standpoint, we become owners of the other person. Loss of the loved person, no matter how it occurs, is also experienced as loss of an important, valued part of ourselves. In a sense, our value has been lessened or tarnished. Lowered self-worth or self-image is the result.

Most survivors experience loss of self-worth during bereavement, especially if the decedent was an important source of support. The survivor can be troubled by thoughts like: "What am I going to do without him," "I can't make it alone," "I'll never be able to do the things he did," or "There will never be another person who could love me the way he did."

It makes intuitive sense, perhaps, that suicide would result in the survivor's loss of self-worth more than any other form of bereavement. Several features of suicide survivorship make loss of self-worth more certain. First of all, the survivor might be unable to fully relieve herself of responsibility in the decedent's decision to perform suicide, thus increasing her guilt. Guilt strains any sense of esteem a person holds for herself.

Second, we commonly resolve guilt by making atonement or amends or by suffering punishment. Since making amends directly with the decedent is out of the question, the survivor can have unconscious desires to seek punishment. Any sense of deserving retribution leads to further loss of self-worth.

Third, perceiving ourselves to have failed in any endeavor results in a reduction of the value we places on ourselves. If the suicide survivor views herself to have failed for not preventing the suicide, her sense of failure will lead to a loss of self-worth.

* * *

"If you want to really be a failure in life,
have your child commit suicide."

Sue Chance [39]

* * *

Fourth, the factors leading to declines in self-worth are also elements of depression. Depression is more than merely a part of grief; it is also a reaction that results in loss of self-worth. A person who experiences a depression also suffers a loss of esteem.

In addition to these four factors, two more complicated factors assault a suicide survivor's sense of value and self-worth. One comes from the message suicide carries regarding the survivor's "lovableness." As Erich Lindemann and Ina Greer suggested, one way in which we perceive ourselves to be lovable is to believe that the significant people in our lives love us. [40] Implied in this belief is a trust that those who love us will want to be with us and will not deliberately harm, hurt, or injure us.

In intimate relationships of any depth, our value is somewhat enhanced in our own minds by the belief that loved and admired persons also find us worthy of their love, friendship, affection, and approval. Therefore, a significant part of our self-worth normally derives from the knowledge that other people find value or worth in us. Self-worth, then, is partly a reflection of what we see of ourselves because of the way important people react toward us.

When a significant person performs a self-destructive act, the survivor cannot help but take it personally. The implied or obvious message is that the decedent did not care enough about the survivor to want to stay with her. In other words, the decedent did not value the survivor enough to choose life with her rather than death without her. The survivor believes the suicide would not have happened if she had possessed any worth in the decedent's eyes. The act of suicide, therefore, devalues the survivor.

The final way in which suicide detracts from a survivor's sense of worth involves social perceptions. Survivors are keenly aware of society's generally poor appraisal of self-inflicted death. They might think, rightly or wrongly, that people look down upon the decedent for performing suicide, as well as thinking less of the survivor in some way. The decedent loses value in the eyes of others, and perhaps also in the eyes of the survivor.

Any condemnation, whether it comes from the society or the survivor, taints the memories of the once-valued decedent. Consequentially, a decrease in the decedent's value also decreases any worth she might have placed in the relationship with the survivor. A lowering of the decedent's value means a lowering of the survivor's value. Again, the survivor suffers a loss of worth in self.

Perhaps the clearest example of this last phenomenon is the way a child is believed to view suicide. When someone significant in a child's life performs suicide, the child sees the act in one or two different ways. Either leads the child to look upon him or herself as a "bad" person.

In the first case, the child believes the suicide was caused by her own misbehavior. That is, the child made the suicide happen because of her bad behavior. If she had been good and not bad, the significant person would not have decided to suicide. The child can find ample evidence to make this misperception a fact, since parental suicide has to follow a moment of misbehavior that occurred at some point prior to the act. The child gives her own misbehavior incredible power, in fact, the very power to kill the parent or to drive the parent to kill himself.

As might be evident, this reaction of children is very similar to the reaction adults experience when confronted by a suicide. However, children do not possess the rational experience or the psychological sophistication adults have to separate their actions from the actions of others. A child, therefore, personally suffers the consequences brought about by the other's actions. In this case, the child believes an important person completed suicide because he or she was bad. Seeing one's self as "bad" always results in loss of self-worth.

The second way a child perceives herself as "bad" is more complex. Because of the child's own sense of being cheated by the suicide, or because she senses the uncomfortable or outright negative response of others around her toward the suicide, a child might perceive the decedent as a "bad" person. The decedent did a "bad" thing. Since children do not understand atonement, the child will believe that the decedent must he punished to make up for the "bad" thing he or she has done. However, the deceased is no longer around to be punished, even by the child's anger. Therefore, through the process called "identification" (described later), the child internalizes the decedent. The child becomes the "bad" person deserving of punishment. Again, perceiving one's self as bad or deserving of punishment results in loss of personal value, or self-worth.

Even though adults have greater powers of thought and rationalization than children, they lose self-worth in much the same way after a suicide as just described. It is often an epic struggle for the suicide survivor of any age to achieve or regain a healthy appraisal of self.

SELF-DESTRUCTIVE BEHAVIOR

Grief obviously represents a major upheaval in a bereaved person's life. Emotional reactions that are part and parcel of grieving can be so overwhelming that the survivor's will to live becomes dangerously blunted on both physical and psychological levels. In suicide bereavement, increased levels of guilt, blame, and responsibility complicate this matter. The intensity and number of grief reactions experienced, the potential isolation of the survivor, her estrangement from society, and her severe demoralization all result in greater susceptibility to self-destructive behavior.

The survivor's very life might be in jeopardy. For at least a year after a death, all survivors are at risk to take less adequate care of themselves, to become ill, to be hospitalized, to be involved in accidents, or to die or be killed. Arnold J. Toynbee coined the phrase "peril of survivorship" to describe this phenomenon.

Self-destructive tendencies are sometimes apparent. The survivor might feel, consciously or unconsciously, an overwhelming desire to die. While oppressive thoughts of living without the deceased plague the survivor, she might entertain her own suicidal ideas. Among all survivors there are those who attempt to harm themselves or take their own lives and those who succeed in completing suicide.

* * *

"I was drinking way too much, and didn't care. I knew I'd be driving home alone, and made sure to have one more before I left the bar. In the morning, for months, I never knew how I got home the night before,"

A Survivor

* * *

Behaviors not in the best interests of a survivor are not always blatantly self-destructive. All survivors go through periods when they do not take adequate care of themselves. Changes in eating, sleeping, activity, and hygienic habits are common during grief. Increased consumption of coffee, nicotine, alcohol, and prescription drugs is also typical. Nearly all survivors who drive do so, at times, in a preoccupied state of mind, barely aware of any other traffic. In many ways, therefore, the peril of survivorship is a reality regardless of the decedent's cause of death.

The peril of survivorship can be intensified for suicide survivors through another phenomenon called identification. Identification is a psychological term describing how one person takes on characteristics of another person. A tendency has been observed among many survivors to assume and copy various traits of the decedent. These survivors begin to mimic mannerisms, facial expressions, nervous tics, verbal expressions, or behavior patterns once characteristic only of the decedent. Survivors can begin to copy attitudes and thoughts previously expressed by the decedent. Survivors have even been known to develop similar physical symptoms if the decedent was ill prior to the death. The facts speak for themselves. About 40% of individuals who attempt suicide had a parent or relative or friend who had attempted to die by a self-inflicted act.

Just a few survivors demonstrate an extreme example of identification. These survivors report feeling the presence of the deceased inside themselves, seeming as if the decedent's spirit has taken up residence within their bodies.

Identification with the deceased in its ultimate form increases the risk of the survivor repeating the suicide experience. Obsessive focus on the suicidal nature of the death can lead to the survivor's acceptance of, and identification with, the suicidal act. Countless examples illustrate this point.

The number of times identical suicides occur within the same families is an indication that suicide survivors, more than any other survivors, are at greater risk to undertake their own self-destructive course and eventually complete suicide. We need only consider the number of times self-destructive acts are repeated from one generation to the next in a family to understand the power and depth of this risk. A younger brother who drives a car into the same bridge abutment on the anniversary date of an older brother's "accident," a son who takes a gun to his head like his father had done twenty years earlier, or a daughter who overdoses on prescription drugs like her mother before her all serve as examples of identification in its most extreme form.

The insidious influence of identification is also evident among groups of people. Numerous studies and investigations have provided proof that the suicide of one teenager can influence the suicidal thoughts and behaviors of other teenagers. High school freshmen are nearly five times more likely to have thoughts of suicide if a classmate dies by suicide, in contrast to students who have never had a classmate kill him or herself.

"Contagious" or "cluster suicides" are believed to account for as many as 13% of the annual teen suicides. Examples of the outbreak of suicides that periodically plague adolescents include those that occurred in Plano, Texas, in 1983, the Omaha suicides in 1986, suburban Bergenfield, New

Jersey, in March 1987, and Gunn High School in Palo Alto, California, in 2009. The ten suicides of Carmel, California, high school graduates in the 1996 through 2000 classes over an eleven-year period illustrate that the influence of a classmate's suicide continues even after graduation from high school. If there is any doubt about the risks of identification, "mass" suicides like the November 18, 1978, Jonestown suicides of 907 Temple members in Guyana provide a stark example.

Identification with an individual after his death, regardless of its form, is an unconscious attempt on the part of the survivor to hold on to the decedent and to keep him alive. In part, copying traits of the decedent maintains his presence. This allows the survivor to continue to unconsciously deny the reality of the loss.

Identification with the decedent is a very real occurrence; for some survivors, it is a very real risk. Suicide survivors, above all, must remain aware of, and guard against, identification with the decedent's self-destructive behavior. For them, in combination with the peril of survival, identification with the decedent compounds the risk of their own self-destructive actions.

PHYSICAL ILLNESS

Physical health concerns are common among bereaved persons. All survivors are likely to believe their general health is not as good as it was before the death. They more often go to a doctor or hospital after a death than they did before it. Evidence also suggests that there is a relationship between grieving and an increased risk of dying. In other words, a grieving survivor is more likely to die than is a person not under the stress of managing life after the death of someone he or she loved.

Many illnesses experienced by survivors are believed to include psychological components. Such illnesses are often called psychosomatic illnesses. This label carries negative connotations for many people because it suggests to them that the illness is not real, that it has no physical basis, for example caused by a germ or virus, and that it is "all in the head" of the sick person. Therefore, reasonable patients react strongly to being told their physical distress is psychosomatic. Many react just as strongly to hearing someone say, "It's just because you're under a lot more stress."

The psychosomatic diagnosis does not discount the real physical aspects of illness. Psychosomatic illnesses are considered real and are known to have physical determinants and outcomes. The term psychosomatic implies that the origins of illnesses are not always purely natural causes or physical reactions. In fact, psychosomatic illnesses can be physical illnesses resulting from processes having critical psychological components like anxiety, stress, and depression.

* * *

"It was one flu or cold or infection after another, and I just refused to go to a doctor. He didn't get help, why should I?"

A Survivor

* * *

Thomas Holmes and Richard Rahe designed a clinical scale in 1967 for measuring how stress affects health. The scale includes a list of forty-three stressful life events that can contribute to illness, ranked in order of their significance. Each event is assigned a number called "Life Change Units," with the highest score being 100 and the lowest being 11 units. Adding up the units of each event that has occurred in the past year of an individual's life provides a final score used to estimate the person's risk of illness in the next year. Grief appears on The

Social Readjustment Rating Scale in three places. Death of a spouse is at the top, having the highest Life Change score. Death of a close family member is the fifth highest score and death of a close friend is ranked at seventeenth. [41]

Bereavement is obviously a stressful time. After a death, survivors frequently experience physical symptoms indicative of somatic anxiety and stress. For example, survivors complain more frequently of headaches, digestive upsets, asthma, arthritis, colitis, and rheumatism, all of which are stress-related. In their situation, it might be more appropriate to identify these physical ailments as "grief-related" illnesses. If it were not for the death, giving them 37 to 100 Life Change Units, the survivors might not be ill.

Colin Parkes reported that people in grief frequently experience heart palpitations and feelings of fullness in the chest. Both of these reactions are typical symptoms of panic attacks and generalized anxiety. Parkes estimated that three-quarters of the increased death rate during the first six months of bereavement is attributable to heart disease, particularly coronary thrombosis and arteriosclerotic heart disease. [42] These forms of heart disease are frequently linked to elevated, chronic stress levels.

Symptoms of physical declines in health usually develop gradually during bereavement. Naturally, survivors are more fatigued due to sleep loss, reduced appetite, and decreased energy. On top of grief-related symptoms, physical side effects like shaking, nervousness, or intestinal irregularities can result from increased use of alcohol, drugs, tobacco, and caffeinated drinks like coffee and soda. Survivors usually interpret any physical symptom as incomprehensible deterioration in health, rather than correctly attributing it to the grief process.

Suicide survivors are definitely susceptible to grief-related physical illnesses. Along with physical exhaustion, hyperalertness (or jumpiness), and depression, they frequently report migraine headaches, hypertension, colitis, peptic ulcers, panic attacks, and bronchial asthma. However, suicide survivors appear no more apt to seek the help of a doctor than other survivors. Nor do they seek the support of a minister, counselor, therapy group, or psychiatrist during the grief process any more often than do other survivors.

WITHDRAWAL OR ISOLATION

As described in Chapter Three, artificial limits are commonly imposed upon grief by those who interact with the survivor but who themselves do not experience the full intensity of the grief. Friends, acquaintances, coworkers, or other family members signal the survivor, both directly and subtly, that mourning has lasted long enough. This typically seems to happen two to three months after the funeral, sometimes much sooner.

Survivors commonly report someone insisting that "You've got to start getting over this," or "This has gone on long enough," or "He's gone now, you've got to learn to get along without him." More subtle interventions are also encountered. People begin to change the subject of conversation when the survivor talks about the death or the deceased. Some people become too busy to take telephone calls from the survivor, while others show silent, but obvious discomfort when she talks about the grief. Any communication suggesting others have had enough of the bereavement, whether directly or subtly expressed, interferes with the survivor's grief work.

Survivor reactions vary when encountering the efforts of others to prematurely bring grief to a close. In order to make the others more comfortable around her, the survivor might put up a front that things are better in her life. She might take part in frivolous conversation, while inwardly crying out to talk about the decedent. Another survivor might demand that others listen, thereby assuring their increased discomfort and the likelihood they will stay away. A survivor might also isolate herself from anyone who seems troubled by, or tired of the grief.

* * *

> "That was the most traumatizing time in my life. I didn't want to see anyone, talk to anyone, or be with anyone. Being awake at home in a dark room was as much as I could handle."
>
> A Survivor

* * *

Eventually real grieving seems possible only in solitude or with someone who is patient and understanding. The time arrives in nearly all bereavements when the survivor must complete much of the grief work alone.

Any bereavement, regardless of the cause of death, results in some amount of loneliness and isolation. Since few people are comfortable listening to the survivor talk about the death, support for the survivor typically diminishes noticeably after the "official" mourning period. There might be changes in relationships with family members, in-laws, and friends. Friendships developed within the context of the relationship with the decedent are often lost or abandoned. The survivor sometimes feels less socially likable and often feels like a "fifth wheel" or tang-along.

Factors common to suicidal death increase the likelihood of lost social support and isolation among suicide survivors. First of all, suicide survivors commonly hesitate or avoid talking about the death. Family and friends often insist that the survivor not talk about the death, even arguing vehemently that the death was not a suicide. Some friends deliberately avoid the survivor. Then, some people point at the survivor, blaming her for the suicide.

The general cultural distaste for suicide often results in decreased availability of support normally offered to survivors. Additionally, since a large segment within our society views suicide as a shameful act, survivors learn to avoid others who express or hold judgmental attitudes. This outcome has become predictable to researchers. Kjell E. Rudestam reported that, when asked about a relative who had died by suicide, nearly half of the people did not want to discuss the event. Nearly one-third of the survivors hedged about the death, describing it as an accident or natural death. [43] The embarrassment and stigmatization experienced by individuals who were in close relationships with the decedent are discussed in Chapter 7.

In the end, a great number of suicide survivors characteristically isolate themselves in order to cope with guilt, anger, shame, and the perception of stigma associated with suicide. Greater withdrawal or isolation by a survivor in various uncomfortable, even distressing, circumstances after a suicide is understandable.

IDEALIZATION

Memories of what was good and pleasant to the survivor in the relationship with the decedent have special meaning. The rewarding and comfortable aspects of that relationship, no matter how little there might have been, are what the survivor will miss most of all. The survivor's attention and preoccupation, therefore, will naturally focus upon this significant aspect of the loss. Yet, for mourning to be successfully completed, the survivor must attain a realistic perception of the decedent's humanness, faults and all.

Grief is only partially complete if the survivor clings to her memories of the decedent's finer qualities, as if remembering unpleasant parts of the relationship is somehow threatening. Admitting to unpleasant parts of a relationship can be an arduous task. Of course, every survivor has memories of the decedent's faults, failings, and weaknesses and the troubles within the relationship, but there seems to be a natural tendency to avoid thinking and speaking about them. The guilt, remorse, and anger with which the survivor is already struggling contribute to this difficulty. Acknowledging negative aspects of either the decedent or the relationship potentially increases the intensity of these troubling emotions.

Unpleasant memories regarding the decedent are also often repressed at a deep psychological level. The imperative to not speak ill of the dead has ancient roots and remains an internal psychological taboo and social rule of proper behavior. It just seems unfair and disloyal to talk about anything but the pleasant memories when someone has died.

Honest consideration of all aspects of the relationship and characteristics of the decedent becomes more likely as grief progresses. Troublesome emotions are slowly resolved and the survivor's psychic energy begins to replenish. At this later point, the need to defend against ill thoughts toward the deceased usually begins to diminish.

If a survivor's guilt and emotional pain regarding the death are severe enough, she tends to continue avoiding negative thoughts about the decedent. When a survivor feels safe to only recall positive aspects of the relationship, the deceased can become idealized in the survivor's perception. This is similar to being granted "sainthood."

Elevating the decedent's status is not seriously counterproductive to bereavement unless the survivor internalizes the idealized image, devoid of human frailties. Internalization of an idealized image creates a mental scale against which the survivor will make future comparisons of herself and others. Since the internalized ideal image presents an impossible standard to be measured against, the scales of comparison tip heavily in favor of the idealized decedent. Later, the survivor might discover increasing difficulty accepting common human faults within herself and others. Ultimately, the grief process can be thwarted, and recovery, as demonstrated in the formation of healthy and rewarding new relationships, is obstructed.

Suicide survivors do not necessarily idealize the decedent, but often do find it hard to acknowledge his human faults. The survivor's wish to deny the truth regarding the suicidal circumstances of the death contributes significantly to this difficulty.

The culturally-determined negative judgment regarding suicide makes it nearly impossible for the survivor to consider the suicidal act as anything but "bad" or abnormal. When an act is considered bad, there is a natural inclination to also consider the one who performs it to be bad. Therefore, to judge suicide bad is also to judge the decedent bad. This puts the suicide survivor in a tenuous and unenviable position. Denying the suicidal nature of the death and avoiding negative thoughts about the deceased lead to, and reinforce each other. This circular reaction prevents honest appraisal of the relationship and the deceased. It also nearly guarantees unfinished grief work.

The difficulty suicide survivors face in acknowledging unpleasant memories can also be attributed to the greater intensity of guilt and anger reactions they often experience. Consideration of the decedent's failings can be dangerous if it triggers anger, because that invariably results in an intense surge of additional guilt. In current learning theory terms, the survivor experiences this guilt surge as a sort of punishment for thinking less than good thoughts about the decedent. To avoid these punishing sequences, the survivor expends a great deal of energy to avoid negative thoughts about the decedent.

Attempting to avoid further guilt in this way prevents seeing the decedent's humanness honestly and accepting it in its entirety. As just suggested above, a likely result is that the grief process will be short-circuited and the survivor will be stuck in grief. Ultimately, denying the nature of the suicidal death and avoiding the articulation of anything but fine and glowing remarks about the decedent can continue throughout the remainder of the survivor's life.

LOSS OF LIBIDO

Levels of human energy are closely tied to what we consider to be appetites. For example, we eat food to take in nutrients in order to generate the energy necessary to take actions that match intentions and propel us toward our goals. Actions use up the energy that must then be replenished, signaled by the sense of appetite. *Libido* is a term used in some psychological theories to denote psychic and emotional energy associated to basic human instincts and appetites, especially the sex drive.

Bereavement brings with it a disturbing upset to human drives and appetites. The survivor's characteristic needs, urges, and drives, and the behaviors expressive of them, are torn and scrambled. A survivor might find it impossible to go to sleep or might sleep for long periods of the day and night. She might be unable to eat or might endlessly devour food with no interest in what is being ingested. The survivor might also become compulsively hyperactive or might be paralyzed by lethargy and listlessness.

Similarly, uncharacteristic sexual appetites can assail survivors. In some instances, an individual can be troubled by sexual stirrings erupting as early in the grief process as during the funeral arrangements. Some survivors report experiencing an acute sexual longing early in the bereavement that usually is experienced as a temporary reaction.

Acting upon sexual longings sometimes develops into a pattern of promiscuity. More than a desire for sexual fulfillment or satisfaction, it becomes a way for the survivor to avoid the pain of grief. Excessive sexual activity early in bereavement might also reflect the survivor's needs to bolster diminished self-image, to instill hope for a satisfying future, and to vent anger, hostility, and aggression toward the decedent.

The contrast is an almost complete blunting of sexual desire and drive that develops as bereavement progresses. Survivors often fear they have become frigid or impotent, which is rarely, if ever, the case. Considering the number and intensity of emotional reactions suddenly confronting the survivor, that her sexual libido would be drained is not remarkable. In fact, such reactions to grief like psychic numbing, shock, and depression almost always have the impact of lowering sexual desire and expression. As grieving progresses, most survivors will recognize a rekindling of sexual drives.

When sexual feelings revitalize, acting upon them is not always comfortable or feasible. This is true for some suicide survivors. After a suicide, many survivors experience a loss of trust in themselves and in other people. Fear of intimacy often develops and endures for long periods. Consequently, loss of trust and fear of intimacy can blunt both the drive to engage in sexual activity and the capacity to perform such activity.

How soon into the grief process the survivor is able to engage in characteristic sexual activity depends greatly on the efficiency of the grief work. If emotional reactions are dealt with and resolved, sexual drives and desires usually return little changed from their state prior to the death. For some survivors this might occur within a few months. For others, years pass before the critical grief work is completed and sexuality can be expressed normally.

Suicide Bereavement Is More Than Common Grief

In greater part, suicide bereavement is the same as other bereavements. All survivors, regardless of the cause of death, normally experience the grief reactions described in this chapter. As common grief reactions, they also comprise a significant part of suicide bereavement. If there is a difference in them at all within suicide bereavement, it is the intensity of their impact upon the survivor. Evidently, some grief reactions, like guilt, that are not typically serious in other bereavements, might reach severe levels within suicide bereavement.

As suggested earlier, there is more to grieving a suicide than is common in other bereavements. Suicide survivors also experience special grief reactions resulting from special aspects of death by suicide. These include the unexpected nature of the death, the fact that death occurs by other-than-natural cause, and the all too evident fact that the death was self-inflicted. The special reactions encountered by suicide survivors are described in the following three chapters.

six

Because Suicide Can Be So Unexpected

"While it may not be possible to say that one kind of loss is more painful than the other, the trauma of unanticipated loss is clearly the more disabling."
Colin Parkes and Robert Weiss [44]

Suicide is sudden and unexpected death. Even when previous suicide threats or attempts are experienced, most people do not believe death will occur by suicide. Very few suicide survivors are prepared for death, let alone a suicidal death.

Death is traumatic even when anticipated. Yet, knowing in advance that a death is probable or imminent gives the survivor time to prepare for the trauma. It seems to help the survivor understand it. Knowing in advance also allows her to begin redefining both her concept of self and her life apart from the decedent before the death actually happens. Anticipation, therefore, is an important determinant of the survivor's ability to accept the death and to achieve recovery.

In contrast, Parkes and Weiss maintained that survivors of unexpected death often dwell on what happened and search desperately for reasons to explain the death. They concluded that unanticipated death, regardless of its cause, results in the most severe bereavement reactions.

Unexpected death occurs in many forms, including accidents, homicides, suicides, heart attacks, renal failures, tumors, hemorrhages, and other natural causes. Survivors experiencing sudden and unexpected death must deal with special grief reactions in addition to the common grief reactions following any loss. Survivors who have anticipated the death seldom encounter these special reactions.

These special grief reactions are shared by most survivors traumatized by unexpected death, regardless of the cause of the death. Although these reactions are not unique to suicide survivors, since suicide is usually swift and unanticipated, unexpected grief reactions are common additions to suicide bereavement.

Grief reactions that result from unexpected death include an extended search for an explanation, taking responsibility for the death, feeling blamed for the death, vivid memories of the time of death, and resultant dysfunctional relationships.

SEARCH FOR EXPLANATION

Reasonable people look for answers to everything. There must be a reason for events and outcomes. Until the mind settles on a reason, it goes back and forth, considering possibilities, sometimes spinning. Unanswered questions, nagging, haunting, gaping holes in logic, tend to turn into intrusive thoughts that come in unwelcome moments. They disrupt sleep as the person hopes to dream of answers.

Accepting a loved one's death depends on having an acceptable reason for it. Thus, when death occurs, nearly all survivors initially question why the deceased was taken from their lives. The strength and plausibility of available explanations influence the severity and length of the grief experience and determine whether or not the survivor will be able to make sense of the loss.

* * *

"I don't think she really wanted to die. She just couldn't find a way to keep on living."

A Survivor

* * *

Religious and philosophical explanations for death are most likely. For example, accepting death as "God's will," believing God has brought the decedent home, that he rests in God's arms, or has achieved a final reward in heaven are all common acceptable explanations. Survivors also accept philosophical explanations to answer the question of death. Examples include "Death is just the final stage of life," "He is better off away from life's trials," and "Death comes to each of us in our own time."

Additionally, simple rational explanations are often enough to provide the survivor understanding for the death. Examples include "We are all human and must eventually die," "He would never have wanted this to happen," and "Those left behind have to pick up the pieces and go on with their lives."

Survivors who seek a religious answer for a suicide find the search difficult. Religious teachings and beliefs, and therefore the clergy, can be judgmental about self-inflicted death. The beginning of an answer might be found in the Boston/Baltimore Catechism. The Church teaches that God is *omnipotent* (all powerful), *omniscient* (all knowing), and *omnipresns* (all present). The last one is important in its interpretation. God, being omnipresent, is everywhere and in all things at the same time. In this one word, religion instructs that there is "no place where God is not." In a religious framework, then, that means that God is in all forms of death, including suicide.

Realistically, grief is not an expression of concern for the decedent. It does not result from a belief that the decedent is suffering in death or is worse off for having died and left life behind. Grief is a process of dealing with a loss to self. The pain of grief is that an important part of the survivor's life has been completely and irretrievably snatched away. And, there must be an acceptable reason for "why" the pain has arrived at the survivor's door. Therefore, the search for an acceptable answer for the decedent's death is more a search for the reason for the survivor's painful loss, and the mental effort is an effective outlet for the "self-pity" normal in bereavement.

Among survivors prepared for death, the search for an explanation is usually not a serious concern and does not occupy a major portion of the survivor's attention. It is commonly resolved early in the bereavement. This is so, in part, because these survivors suffer through a portion of their grief and resolve some of their self-pity before the death. Also, these survivors have had time prior to the death to reach acceptable reasons for it.

Unexpected death results in a search for answers that is more intense, more solitary, and more difficult to complete than follows anticipated death. Common explanations, whether religious, philosophical, or rational, are not so easily accepted when death comes swiftly. Survivors unprepared for death deny its reality for longer periods of time than those expecting the death. Sudden death also often appears to the survivor to have been preventable. Consequently, accepting any answer for their own suffering takes a longer time and a harder course.

Among suicide survivors, looking for reasons for the death is a significant and critical grief reaction. It occupies a great deal of the survivor's time, energy, and attention. It can go on for years after the death, and sometimes is never satisfactorily resolved. Edwin Shneidman believed that a suicide sentences survivors "to obsessing about the reasons for the suicide death." [45]

Part of the survivor's difficulty is that the search for explanation after suicide is invested with guilt. As described in Chapter Five, these survivors often encounter a more intense form of guilt than other survivors. Their search for explanation, therefore, is not just a search to answer why the loss to self must be suffered, it is also, in large measure, an examination of the relationship to determine how much responsibility she shares for the suicide.

The search for explanation is made all the more challenging because of the nature of suicidal death. The decedent *chose to die*. Neither the survivors nor those who seek to comfort them can disregard the self-inflicted element of the death. The question "Why?" is so apparently on everyone's mind, that it becomes pervasive and overwhelming. The questions seem far weightier than the possible answers, and the survivor is often left to discover what answers she can alone.

Suicide survivors seek out answers wherever they can be found: from clergy, counselors, medical doctors, support groups, librarians, and Web sites. Those fortunate to discover an acceptable answer move toward successful resolution of their grief.

There have been cultures in which explanations for suicide were socially acceptable. In several eastern cultures, if a person intent on regaining his honor performed suicide, it was considered a noble act. Romans no longer able to maintain pleasant, productive, or dignified lives, were free to end their lives without moral, legal or religious condemnation. Norsemen who had grown too old or infirm to fight or who had become social burdens performed acceptable and noble suicides. In our own culture, soldiers who knowingly sacrifice their own lives for the sake of comrades-in-arms are rendered honored memorials rather than being judged for a self-inflicted fatality.

In the circumstances of normal, day-to-day living, suicide is generally not accepted in our society. There are no romantic Romeo and Juliet suicides, no noble Socrates suicides. Today, suicides are tragic and blameworthy, and someone must be held accountable when they happen.

The particular circumstances surrounding each suicide might be different, but most people consider suicide simply as an escape from some intolerable circumstance. The most common explanations for suicide include fractured love relationships, personal problems, disappointed expectations, financial difficulties, depressions, humiliations, hopelessness, long-endured pain or physical illnesses, and mental illnesses. These explanations for death obviously differ from those society offers other survivors. They are not comforting and the survivor usually does not find them emotionally acceptable.

Those who have not experienced a suicide cannot comprehend the difficulty faced by suicide survivors in arriving at an acceptable explanation for the death. Explaining why a person decides to end his or her life takes time and emotional effort. Typically, the survivors begin the search by dissecting the events and interactions that took place with the decedent just before the death. These events are considered most likely to have *precipitated* the suicidal act, and survivors give them a special power that is not ordinary. Survivors also tend to focus on actions they might have neglected to take to change the decedent's mind.

Although "precipitating events" are overemphasized and laden with mythical qualities, they almost always prove to be inadequate explanations for the suicide. On a rational level, no one really believes a person decides to take her own life because angry words were spoken, a meal was burned, a date was forgotten, a bank account was overdrawn, the car fender was dented, a lover left without a kiss goodbye, a promotion fell through, or any of the other myriad reasons often considered to explain suicide. A survivor seldom finds an acceptable reason among them.

As Karl Menninger said, "What is characteristic of a very large number of suicides is the apparent inadequacy of the precipitating event [as an explanation for its occurrence]." [46] The survivors must look elsewhere for the solution, since precipitating events do not usually satisfactorily answer the question, "Why?"

A painful reflection of historical events in the life with the decedent follows. The survivor begins looking for past failures shared with the deceased. Events perhaps years old are subjected to microscopic analysis, all too frequently resulting in sad, and usually unwarranted, conclusions. Many a survivor berates herself with remorseful ruminations like, "If only I had..." or, "If only I had not..."

Looking to the past seldom yields satisfactory answers for the survivor. The problem is that the survivor cannot be detached enough from the relationship to see the facts clearly. Also, few survivors are able to separate their interactions with the decedent from the entire span of the decedent's life course. They do not look far enough into the decedent's past to discover where the roots of the suicidal death likely began. Consequently, survivors tend to accept responsibility for the suicide.

Realistically, interactions between survivor and decedent are only peripherally implicated in any self-destructive act. The real causes and motivations for suicide are internal and develop throughout a person's life. This helps explain the difficulty of devising satisfactory explanations for the decedent's action after the suicidal event.

Few suicides result from a singular, acute life crisis or event. As William Steele stated, there is no one reason why a person takes his life. The feelings that bring a person to a suicidal crisis result from a series of losses and difficult times. It is the combination of losses and failures that brings most people to the conclusion that life is not worth living. [47]

Suicide is a very complex, multidimensional act that develops over the course of a lifetime. Karl Menninger suggested that the self-destructive tendencies take root very early in a person's life and so strongly influence the entire course of development as to overshadow and finally conquer the opposing instinct to live. He maintained that suicide is an extremely complex reaction to life. It cannot be viewed as a simple act of impulse, whether the act is considered to have been logical or irrational. Nor can suicide "be explained as the result of heredity, suggestion, [insanity], or any of the other symptoms of maladjustment that so frequently precede it. Rather, we are frequently able to see the steady progression of self-destructive tendencies first appearing long before the consummation of the critical act." [48]

Similarly, Ronald Maris suggested that most individuals who die by suicide have historically made self-destructive adaptations to life's circumstances. He pointed out that suicides tend to have greater accumulated developmental burdens and stresses than people who do not complete suicide. Maris considered suicide to be a product of gradual loss of hope and the will and resources to live. It is "a kind of running down and out of life energies, a bankruptcy of physic defenses against death and decay." [49]

John Hewett included an "Explanations That Make Sense" section in his book. He describes the despair, the feeling of being "trapped in a corner by this overwhelming and unbearable mental pain" that individuals dealing with suicidal thoughts and ideas encounter. [50]

Ideas like running down and out of life energies, a bankruptcy of physic defenses, and the emergence of despair hint at a common foundation for later suicidal actions. *Resilience* is a similar concept.

The common belief that "children are resilient" is based on the observations that children can experience and survive personal challenges early in their development. Resilience implies that a child can "bounce back" from stress and adversities. Rather than being overwhelmed by childhood life, boys and girls tap into the resilience within and find ways to overcome hardships. Instead of giving in to, or capitulating to, unwelcome circumstances, they look for ways to get beyond the status quo when finding themselves in situations not to their liking.

Diligent striving is another term for resilience. [51] *Striving* becomes apparent in a child's efforts to meet challenges, to better herself and her situation, to improve her performance, to accomplish goals and objectives, and to be undeterred by risk. The *diligent* part of *diligent striving* is most relevant in order to understand a child's actions whenever he or she is under duress of any kind. Persevering and constant in effort, children who are diligent seldom give up. Diligence is an aspect of bravery—to continue endeavoring toward the objective no matter the odds, obstacles, or setbacks. The story of Jim Day in Chapter Four is an example of this characteristic.

One more term is helpful here. *Endurance* is a personal quality related to patient sufferance and lasting resilience. The quality is demonstrated in working long and hard without stopping, even in the face of difficult situations or pain. The meaning of "long," of course, varies according to the type of exertion required to "keep on." To demonstrate endurance, there must obviously be something to endure, and depression is one of those *somethings*. Over time, chronic depression is an experience that challenges and tests an individual's limits. For many seriously depressed individuals getting through a day can be more than a challenge, it can become insurmountable.

Growing beyond childhood and adolescence requires a good amount of resilience. The reality is, however, that all humans are not born with the same reservoir of resilience. Children of the same age in the same circumstances strive diligently in different degrees. And, if resilience ever runs out, life and activity come to a halt. If the mind and body cannot recover or regenerate resilience, death will arrive in one form or another. Like a man lost and wondering for hours in a blizzard, trudging through knee-deep snow drifts, there comes a point where the body will push on no further, and sitting down and waiting becomes the only option, no matter how much the exhausted man wants to continue.

When someone believes there is no meaning in his/her life, that her existence is a burden on those who love her, and that the pain she has always borne will never go away, it requires much endurance and diligent striving to get through each day. When sleep brings no restoration, and when waking to another day that seems to hold nothing is unwelcome, not waking for another day seems to make sense. When exhausted and depleted of resilience, to a person unable to recover life energies and physic defenses, sitting down and waiting for another day can make even less sense.

Suicide survivors often turn to books in their search for answers. Among the many available research and literary efforts to explain why suicide occurs are: Herbert Hendin's *Suicide in America*, [54] Kay Redfield Jamison's *Night Falls Fast: Understanding Suicide*, [55] and George Howe Colt's *November of the Soul: The Enigma of Suicide*. [56] Edwin Shneidman succinctly summarized the difficulties involved in the suicide survivor's search for explanation, the search for the "why" of an individual suicide. He stated that "the causes of suicide are multiple and terribly complex and remain one of the great enigmas of human nature." [57]

In the end, explanations for a suicide are to be found only within the individual who chooses self-destruction. According to Alfred Alvarez, "each suicide has its own inner logic and unrepeatable despair." [52] No matter how intimate the relationship, no one is privy to the inner workings of another's emotions, thought processes, and unconscious drives. As Menninger rightfully concluded, an understanding of the motives to complete suicide is made difficult not only because the motives that seem obvious are most untrustworthy, but also because "a successful suicide is beyond study." [53]

Finally, the explanations for death usually shared among mourners and comforters do not fit the circumstances of a death by suicide. There is little comfort for suicide survivors in remarks like, "It was meant to be," "His time had come," "It was God's will," "He is happier now with God," and "There was nothing more you could have done." All seem inappropriate and are seldom offered.

Ultimately in the survivor's search, there will be no real "explanation" for why the decedent completed suicide. The reasons are always hidden within the decedent—lost forever in the act of self-destruction chosen. Explanations cannot he derived from the analysis of everyday interactions or isolated events.

The hope for the survivor is that she or he will, as much as possible, relieve her/himself of any burden of responsibility and accept the suicide as a choice made alone, for whatever reason, by the decedent.

TAKING RESPONSIBILITY

When death happens unexpectedly, there is a nagging perception that it could have been prevented, avoided, or somehow postponed. Very often, the survivor takes responsibility for not preventing the death.

Survivors of unexpected death assume undue responsibility for the death in several ways. The most troubling for any survivor is the perception that she somehow directly caused it. Another is the belief that the survivor could have or should have prevented the death. There might also be a sense that the survivor should have been aware that death was imminent instead of being surprised by it.

Perhaps more than any survivor of unexpected death, the suicide survivor is likely to experience an overwhelming sense of responsibility in the decedent's death. The survivor might feel that she drove the decedent to despair or desperation. Nearly all feel they should have at least been aware of the decedent's suicidal intent and acted to prevent the death. This is especially true if the decedent had ever communicated suicidal intent.

The idea of shared responsibility for suicidal death is rooted in social attitudes. As previously noted, our culture provides no adequate or acceptable explanations for death by suicide. The survivor usually searches independently for reasons and is likely to discover ways in which she appears to be responsible for the suicide.

Suicide survivors usually focus on personal actions or minor omissions that appear to have motivated the decedent's self-destructive act. As Goldberg and Mudd suggested, the self-inflicted death is often hostile and loaded with the implication that the survivor is somehow at fault. The survivor, after the fact, finds it almost impossible to ignore this accusation. [58]

Cultural beliefs generate further difficulties for the suicide survivor. Current social attitudes stress that suicides can be and should be stopped. In other words, if a suicide could have been prevented, it should have been. This pervasive attitude places the responsibility for suicide prevention outside the decedent. This means the responsibility for the decedent's action belongs to someone else.

* * *

"If I'd gone over there when she called, she'd be alive right now. I'm sure of that."

A Survivor

* * *

As Gerald Ginsburg stated, many people believe the responsibility to see that suicide attempts do not occur or reoccur lies particularly within the family. Therefore, there is a greater tendency among suicide survivors to take responsibility for either causing the death, or for not preventing it, than is experienced in any other bereavement.

The difficulty with attitudes and beliefs that place the responsibility for suicide outside the decedent is they disregard the inherent realities of self-destruction. These beliefs essentially ignore facts that many in the suicide prevention profession have recognized. The truth about suicide is that, when a person decides to take her own life, fully intends to die, and has the lethal method at hand, there is little to nothing another person can do to prevent that particular suicide. Also, if a person has given up all hope for life, she will evade every effort to save her life and take the first opportunity to bring it to an end.

If there is doubt about this, it is illuminating to consider Ronald Maris' contention that 75% of those who complete suicide do so in their first attempt.[59] Is it because the survivor didn't respond to the crisis quickly or efficiently enough that so many people successfully end their lives, or is it because the decedents' intent to die is strong enough that they select a time and method for their death in which intervention is impossible? The July 17, 1989 *Time Magazine* reported that 64%

of the men and 40% of the women who killed themselves in 1986, did so with firearms. Of the 464 gun fatalities reported in the week of May 1–7, 1989, 216 (47%) were suicides. Some of these individuals shot themselves in the presence or close proximity of other family members. The use of a gun in a suicide strongly implies the intended finality of the action. Lethal methods like guns usually remove the chance of a lifesaving change of mind, discovery, or rescue—even when those who might stop the suicide are present.

The true responsibility for the suicide lies with the decedent, not the survivor. If this fact evades the survivor, the consequence of the generally-accepted, social belief that suicide should be prevented is that she can never, with any great assurance, conclude whether or not her actions might have made a difference in the completion of the other's death.

There is another feature of assuming responsibility for the death few survivors, other than suicide survivors, experience. It is associated with searching for an explanation: the importance of clues. After the death, most suicide survivors search for clues that might have indicated before the suicide that it was going to happen. Most discover them, both obvious and subtle. With clues uncovered, survivors castigate themselves for not being sensitive enough to notice the clues in time and for not doing something about the risk their loved one was facing.

Unfortunately for the survivor, this hindsight is given far too much power. For one thing, the relationship between the survivor and decedent is usually too close for the survivor to be able to perceive a clue for what it is at the time it happens. For another, even if the survivor might have been acutely aware of the decedent's suicidal potential, only in exceptional cases does a survivor believe that a suicide will occur. Most individuals, regardless of the seriousness of the circumstances and the anxiety they feel, cannot anticipate self-inflicted death nor believe it might happen.

Clues certainly occur. However, their authority in predicting a suicide is mythical. We all experience in our interactions with others many of the clues that "predict" suicide. We encounter others who are depressed, hopeless, despairing, or unusually euphoric, who give their prized things away, who say strange goodbyes, or who write troubling or confused notes or letters. In most cases, such clues are not followed by suicide, and they hold no particular significance. We think little of them in retrospect.

It is only in hindsight, when a suicide has occurred, that clues aggregate their demonic power. The belief in clues serves no helpful purpose for the survivor. Ultimately, this belief serves only to increase the survivor's tormenting struggle to be relieved of responsibility in the death.

FEELING BLAMED

"If it weren't for you he'd still be alive!"

Sudden death in our society seems to imply that the decedent was in some sort of stressful or frustrated state, and attitudes toward the death and the survivor are sometimes judgmental or punitive. This is true whether the death was by natural cause, accident, homicide, or suicide.

When death comes unexpectedly, shock is intensified for both the survivor and others around her. An early need in the bereavement is to assign a causal explanation for the death in order to make sense of the loss. As described above, it is more difficult to understand and accept unexpected death. Also, the survivor assumes some responsibility for the loss. These reactions to unexpected death can trigger a sense of blame for the death in the survivor. Troubling enough as it is, the survivor also often encounters obvious blame from others. Such outright blame for the death usually comes from family and friends of the deceased.

Casting blame is probably the consequence of a need to find a "scapegoat" for sudden death. Someone must be at fault when a person suddenly dies without a warning, especially if the decedent was young and healthy.

The survivor does not necessarily encounter blame from others to feel blamed. Normal guilt, need for an explanation, and taking responsibility, can all result in the survivor feeling blameworthy. Such sensitivities make the survivor vulnerable to misinterpreting remarks, facial expressions, and gestures of others. The survivor, then, might naturally assume others consider her at fault, whether they do or not.

Feeling blame increases the suicide survivor's burden of grief unnecessarily. Just as it is inappropriate to attribute the suicide to a single cause, it is inappropriate to assign blame for the death to anyone but the decedent. Edward Dunne and Karen Dunne-Maxim stated it clearly; it seems inappropriate to single out and blame any other person as the agent of a suicide, whether it is a parent, sibling, spouse, lover, friend, or therapist. They give responsibility for the suicide to no one but the decedent. In their words, "the failure to choose life is the failure of the deceased, not of the survivors." [60]

Blame, whether blatant, implied, or imagined, is one bereavement feature unexpected death survivors experience almost exclusively. There is little evidence at this time to indicate if blame is intensified for suicide survivors beyond that experienced by other unexpected death survivors. It is safe to say, however, that experiencing blame for the suicide in some way is a common and consistent aspect of suicide bereavement.

VIVID MEMORIES OF THE DEATH

All survivors have memories of things that occurred at the time of the death. Such memories usually include the day, date, time, and place of the death. Most survivors also very clearly remember where they were and what they were doing when they learned of it. The moment of being told of the death is frequently recalled as if captured on a photograph. Survivors remember the surroundings, the sight, smell, feel, and sound of that moment, in clear detail long years after the death. As time passes, some memories fade. Years later, for example, a survivor might be less clear of the date or not think so much of the time the death happened.

How vivid such memories of the death remain is partly determined by several factors. These include the circumstances surrounding the death, anticipation of the death, and whether or not the survivor was present at the death. Survivors present at an expected death that occurs by natural cause and in which the decedent did not suffer painful or traumatic complications are least troubled by vivid recollections of the moment. If the death was difficult for the decedent, even the memories of expected natural death can be vivid and enduring for the survivor. Memories of the time of death are also complicated for these survivors if they were informed of it afterwards instead of being present for the natural death.

Unexpected death survivors are not usually present when the death occurred, rather they are informed of it afterwards. The memory of that event, of being told the death has taken place, is likely to be imprinted vividly upon the survivor's mind. The shock of it fixes the details of that moment into sharp contrast with the "every-day" events that preceded it. For years afterwards, especially around the anniversary of the death, the survivors are likely to experience vivid recollections of being informed of the death. When they describe the details of that event, it is as if it had just recently happened. The memory of the time of death obviously does not fade as readily among survivors of unexpected death. Among suicide survivors it does not seem to fade at all.

Some accident survivors and nearly all suicide survivors experience an additional element to this reaction. This is especially true for survivors who witnessed the suicide or who found the decedent's body. Not only does the time of these events become vivid memories for these survivors, the memories assume painful and troublesome proportions. Troublesome memories seem most frequent among suicide survivors, some of whom experience difficult memories as frequently as daily or weekly.

Suicide survivors report becoming nervous, anxious, depressed, sad, or somehow agitated every day at the hour coinciding with the time of death or of being informed of it. Some become uneasy weekly on the day the death occurred, for example, every Saturday afternoon.

Suicide survivors also report difficulty in returning either to the place where the death happened or where they were when they learned of the suicide. This strong response to the death often means the survivor will move to a new locale immediately. Some are never able to go back into the house, walk into the basement, sleep in the bedroom, or go out to the garage if that is where the suicide occurred. There are also survivors who quit jobs or request transfers because they are unable to again feel at ease in the place they were informed of the death.

A survivor can find these vivid memories so painful and disturbing that she expends great efforts to avoid them. Typically, such efforts imbue the memories with even more emotional power and make them all the more threatening when the survivor can no longer keep them shut out.

* * *

"Just about every night, even now after two years, I'm there. The gun shot, the last breath, the blood, the smells."

A Survivor

* * *

The impact of unexpected death and the added characteristics of suicidal death make this event in the survivor's life one of the most traumatic a person might ever experience. Remembering the moment of death or of being informed of it can elicit strong emotions from the suicide survivor years after the death.

DYSFUNCTIONAL RELATIONSHIPS

A "functional" relationship is one that fosters the emotional, spiritual, psychological, mental, and physical welfare of both of the individuals involved. It ultimately functions to enhance the well-being and survival of both. A functional relationship "works" to the advantage of the persons who invest in it.

In contrast, a "dysfunctional" relationship is one that, in some important way, does not foster an involved person's healthy development. It works against the person, discouraging, detracting from, and undermining his or her healthy and balanced welfare.

Bereavement is a transitional state of existence. It is a period in which the survivor moves from being the person she was in relationship to the decedent to becoming the person she will be having lost a significant part of herself. While grief progresses, changes in the survivor's relationships are frequent. Some relationships are strengthened. Yet, grief can tax and threaten any relationship, whether it is with a family member, friend, or work associate. How relationships weather the storm of grief depends on a mix of factors, including on how the survivor transits her bereavement, on the personality of the survivor, on the quality of the relationships she experienced before the death, and on the understanding of the others toward the survivor after the death.

A suicide survivor brings intense grief reactions into her relationships. Otherwise comfortable relationships can he stressed and challenged to the breaking point as the survivor copes with anger, guilt, depression, blame, feeling responsible, and trying to explain the suicide. A troubled or conflict-ridden relationship can be expected to come apart at the seams as sparks turn into major fireworks.

There might be a greater tendency for survivors of unexpected death to experience dysfunctional relationships afterwards, compared with survivors having had an opportunity to prepare for the death. This, perhaps, results from the basic difference in the two bereavements.

Survivors expecting death have time to prepare for the loss of the relationship. Preparing for the death includes anticipation of the loss of satisfactions and gratifications of the relationship. When the death occurs, the shock of its loss is not quite as devastating, and the survivor does not cling so desperately to the relationship.

Whether or not other relationships survive the bereavement, survivors generally eventually return to thinking, behaving, and feeling in ways similar to before the death. Of course, there is a part of the survivor that will never be the same—the part that had been shared with the decedent.

How significant the part of self lost after a death becomes depends partially on how individualized the survivor was within the relationship with the decedent. This, in turn, affects how long grief endures. A survivor who had been very dependent upon the decedent will take longer to complete the grief work than a person who had been able to achieve and maintain a healthy level of independence and individualization within the relationship.

Many survivors who have already accomplished much of the grief work before entering a new relationship are fortunate enough to build relationships that help in completing the grief work and moving back into an adequately functioning life.

Spouses, lovers, and partners are especially at risk for developing dysfunctional relationships after a suicide. Understandably, survivors of sudden death experience strong urges to fill the empty spot left by the death. They also, quite naturally, desire to escape from or to be rescued from the painful complex of emotions that grief brings. Some survivors respond by replacing the lost relationship with a new one. In fact, unfulfilled needs sometimes push the survivor to seek out new relationships during bereavement. Unexpected death is a sudden and pitiless severance of a relationship, like stripping away living flesh from the survivor's frame, and one way to anesthetize the pain of such loss is to replace the lost relationship with another. Relationships, even those that had been established before the death, are a risky business at this time.

As stated above, the survivor is going through a transition. She will not return entirely to being her former self, nor can she know who she will become when the grief process has been completed. Unfortunately, relationships developed within the first year or two of bereavement are usually founded upon unhealthy psychological complexes. These factors primarily operate on an unconscious level well beneath the survivor's awareness, and interfere with her perceptions and judgments.

Most survivors are incapable of objectively perceiving the state they are in while deluged with grief's strong emotions. Thus, the survivor is not likely to be in a psychological state facilitating beneficial and satisfying choices. Relationships that do not work for the survivor are likely. Many, but not all, relationships formed during this period are neither functional nor long lasting and seem doomed to flounder.

Frequently, relationships established during bereavement follow somewhat predictable patterns. Some survivors involve themselves with someone who seems remarkably similar to the decedent, while others find themselves with someone who seems the complete opposite. Other survivors involve themselves in repetitious relationships.

Each of these choices is fraught with emotional difficulties, because, in many ways, they represent an attempt by the survivor to bring an artificial end to grief.

The problem with a relationship with someone apparently similar to the decedent is that the new relationship is not really a replacement of the old relationship, but is more a continuance of it. This seems to reflect a tendency on the survivor's part to select a person in whom the old complaints and problems of the prior relationship are repeated. Thus, the new relationship is at once an old and familiar one, grounded in part by an unconscious wish not only to have the decedent back but also to deny that the death ever happened. It is as if the survivor says to herself, "See nothing is different. He's still here. Nothing has changed. He's not dead."

The dynamics of repetitious relationships are complex. The choice of a "carbon copy" partner is largely determined by unconscious motivations and decisions. In other words, the survivor forms the relationship without actually knowing or understanding why. The premature substitution of one partner for another indicates, in part, that the grief work consequent to the loss of the first relationship was incomplete. Repetitions occur, because the reactions to the original loss and the personal issues that had been operative in that relationship had not been adequately resolved by the survivor.

Multiple marriages can provide an example of the nature of repetitious relationships. Those who have studied multiple marriages have found that a survivor of one marriage often selects someone who is "just like the first one" for a second or third partner. This is apparent in marriages in which alcoholism was an issue. It is not uncommon that a marriage to a spouse trapped in alcoholism, finally severed by death or divorce, is then followed by a marriage to another alcoholic. Interestingly and well beyond the awareness of a spouse, researchers concluded long ago that a strong relationship exists with alcohol, depression, and suicide. Morris E. Chafetz and H. W. Demone, for example, noted that alcohol placed in the hands of some is a "slow form of suicide."[61]

As defined above, dysfunctional relationships are those that do not work well for the survivor. Alcoholic relationships are one example; grief-stricken relationships can prove to be another.

Survivors who form relationships with a person unlike the decedent are trying to facilitate separation from the decedent. Below conscious levels, the survivor concludes a person unlike the decedent might help her to avoid thinking about the decedent. This relationship becomes a defensive repression of grief. Large adjustments are required in forming any new relationship. Doing so with someone unlike the decedent almost ensures that adjustments will be continuous. The survivor will be faced with countless comparisons that threaten to return the focus back upon the deceased. This makes adjustments within the new relationship confusing. Continuous adjustments of this sort also steal away from the time, effort, and energy that would be better directed toward completing the grief work. Incomplete bereavement and a troubled relationship often result.

One danger exists among suicide survivors that other unexpected death survivors seldom face when the decedent was a spouse. Similar to survivors of alcoholic dyads, a small number of suicide survivors tend to substitute the decedent with another person who demonstrates a proclivity toward suicide. This substitution might reflect an unconscious attempt to relieve guilt for omissions in the relationship and for failing to prevent the suicide. In essence, the survivor tries to relieve herself of responsibility for the first suicide by saving another suicidal person from completing a self-destructive course already evident. Potentially, the bereaved suicide survivor is enacting a rescue mission, with objectives to atone for past failures and to affirm her worth and goodness. The survivor proves to self and others that she was not at fault for the first suicide.

In other cases, bereaved survivors experience a series of brief and fruitless relationships, resembling push-pull contests. The survivor desires and needs intimacy, actively courts it, but then draws back from it in fearful alarm. Other survivors isolate themselves and avoid relationships altogether. Both patterns result from a fear of the loss of love and a fundamental loss of trust.

While suffering grief's emotional pains, survivors can find experiencing or expressing feelings of love to be difficult. Some interpret the normal loss of loving feelings during bereavement as an inability to love and worry that the condition is permanent. Proving this fear unfounded often underlies the motivation for entering a new relationship.

Finally, suicide survivors often report feeling a loss of trust, not just in others, but loss of trust in self as well. A survivor questions whether she can trust another person not to do the same thing the decedent did. She also questions her own judgment, her ability to make choices that were so apparently flawed and terribly blind in the previous relationship. She believes, if only for awhile, that she would not have been involved in a relationship ending in suicide if she had been able to judge others adequately in the first place. The experience of suicide in a marriage creates an injury to the survivor's ability to trust, even in others who repeatedly demonstrate that they are trustworthy. This injury must be healed before a survivor can ever feel safe in an intimate relationship again.

Generally, suicide survivors would be well advised to refrain from romantic involvements in at least the first year of bereavement. Unless the survivor is uncommonly lucky, trying to find intimacy and satisfaction in new relationships tends to be troublesome and largely unsuccessful while grief reactions are unresolved and still in process.

Milestones of the grief work must be encountered openly and overstepped successfully. Only after grief's transitional state is eclipsed, only after the survivor is the person she will be apart from the decedent, are fulfilling and prosperous relationships probable.

seven

It Didn't Have To Be This Way

> *"And perhaps there is a limit to the grieving that the human heart can do.*
> *As when one adds salt to a tumbler of water,*
> *There comes a point where simply no more will be absorbed."*
> Sarah Waters, Novelist [62]

On research charts and graphics, death can be divided into a number of categories. The last chapter presented information dividing death into expected and unexpected death. In this short chapter separating death into natural and other-than-natural causes, the survivors' bereavement experiences are again compared.

Two million Americans die each year. Natural causes claim most of those lives. On average, 1,860,000 deaths result from biological, organic, or physical causes like illness, disease, infection, and organ failure. Of the total annual deaths, 140,000 (approximately 7%) result from other-than-natural causes. These untimely deaths include accidents, disasters, homicides, and suicides. Suicide accounts for about 1.5% of the annual deaths in America.

Survivors experience certain distinct grief reactions when death does not result from a natural cause. Accident, homicide, and suicide survivors all deal with these reactions in some degree, whereas survivors of natural death, whether expected or unexpected, seldom experience them.

At the root of these reactions is the belief among other-than-natural death survivors that the death did not have to happen. Deaths occurring by other-than-natural cause present a dilemma to the survivor. Unlike survivors of natural death who can explain, rationalize, and justify the death without great difficulty, other-than-natural death survivors are confronted by an awareness that, had circumstances been somehow different, the death would not have happened. Accident, homicide, and suicide survivors can be plagued by this dilemma for long periods of time throughout the bereavement.

The special other-than-natural grief reactions described in this chapter include viewing the death as preventable, feeling stigmatized by the death, and feeling the decedent deliberately abandoned the survivor. These grief reactions, associated to the belief that the death did not have to happen, add to the suicide survivor's bereavement and are hard to resolve.

PREVENTABLE DEATH

Natural death, even when it occurs suddenly, has a quality of being inevitable. Death from fatal causes, like serious illness, disease, or organ failure, is less confusing to the survivors. Death by cancer or heart attack does not usually present the dilemma of preventability. Even though some physical illnesses and natural deaths can be attributed to the decedent not taking proper or adequate care of him or herself, the majority of natural deaths appear to have been largely unavoidable. Most survivors accept that little beyond divine intervention could have prevented the death.

Other-than-natural death survivors consistently view the death as somehow preventable. Accident, homicide, and suicide survivors all express the belief that the death did not have to happen, that it was not inevitable. Believing the death to have been avoidable adds a troubling "if only…" quality not often found among natural death survivors.

Thoughts and statements of other-than-natural death survivors reflect this quality. Common examples include, "If only he had not gone out that night," "If only I had called her back," "If only he hadn't been there," "If only I had stopped him from leaving," "If only she had waited," "If only it had not rained," or "If only he hadn't bought that gun."

Believing the death to have been preventable is especially prevalent among suicide survivors. The self-inflicted nature of suicide makes it nearly impossible to see the death as anything but preventable. Suicidal death seems preventable in the extreme, because it results from a deliberate act of the decedent.

Accidents and homicides might seem beyond the victim's control. Survivors, therefore, are often able to rationalize the death as strictly circumstantial: that is, the result of external factors or fateful circumstances. Suicide survivors, on the other hand, seldom consider the death circumstantial, and their grief is imbued with an intense "if only" quality expressed in the singularly disquieting statement, "If only he had not killed himself!"

Believing an individual's suicide to have been preventable becomes an obstacle to acceptance of the death and resolution of the grief. The death's "if only" quality is difficult to work through, and survivors tend to expend a great amount of grief energy puzzling over it. Combined with the search for the "why" of the suicide and the survivor's sense of culpability, the "if only" aspect becomes an entangled mess that slows down the grief process considerably in its early stages and is likely to haunt the survivor for many years after the suicide.

STIGMA

The word "stigma" comes from an ancient Greek and Roman practice of burning marks into the skin of criminals and slaves. A stigma was a token of disgrace, reproach, or infamy, indicating a person's social status within the community. The branding mark was considered a visible character reference, giving significant and easily recognizable information about the individual's personality and inclinations to others unfamiliar with him.

Today's application of *stigma* has changed only in the fact that a stigmatized person is not actually subjected to a physical branding on the skin. A stigma today is an invisible wound that burns a person emotionally, psychologically, and mentally.

Stigmatization brings upon a person the feeling of being somehow scarred or marked in a negative or unpleasant way. As in times past, a stigma retains the power to detract from or to permanently damage the reputation of the person stained by it.

* * *

> "The judgment was every place I went. I'd go to the grocery store and see someone staring at me. Whether I knew the person or not, I could see the look on her face. I was damned."
>
> A Survivor

* * *

Survivors of naturally-caused deaths seldom experience a sensation of being scarred or marked by the death. Accident, homicide, and suicide survivors, on the other hand, frequently must deal with the additional grief stress of stigma.

Among suicide survivors, being stigmatized by the death is linked to social beliefs and attitudes about suicide, including their own. Stigma arises from what others around the survivors actually think and from what the survivors believe others think.

Consider that most of the 644 university students introduced in Chapter One, all young adults in an upper level course about understanding suicide and its impact, were born in the early 1980s through the mid-1990s. They grappled with the difficult question, "Would you argue for the belief that death by suicide is normal?" The familiar, unchanging, ingrained attitudes and beliefs that culturally mark suicide as a social taboo and unacceptable are reflected in the answers 361 students (56%) offered over an eleven-year period to support their view that suicide was *not normal*. The persistent beliefs they expressed are summarized below, listed somewhat in the order of how frequently a particular answer was given.

Character of the Decedent: The person would have to be extremely insane, abnormal, or dysfunctional. Normal people do not think of killing themselves. Suicide is the act of a selfish person with a character weakness. It results from the person's laziness and it's just giving up rather than trying. A person would have to be cruel to hurt others by doing this. People who do this are abdicating their purpose and responsibilities, looking for attention, or seeking control. These people just do not care that by killing themselves they are devaluing the lives of others.

Problem Solving: Suicide is taking the easy way out of life's problems. It is an escape and a poor way to get out of problems. What problems does a person solve by killing himself? Suicide is the wrong answer to life problems, because things can always get better. People have other choices for their problems and deliberately dying is not an acceptable option. It doesn't solve anything. It creates more problems than it solves.

Human Nature: Suicide is a strange way to die. It is unnatural and not a natural way to die. Only natural and unplanned deaths are normal, and only natural death should be accepted. Death should never occur on purpose, and suicide is the only death done on purpose. Suicide is the only form of death by choice, and we don't get to choose our fate, it's chosen for us. Suicide is completely contrary to the most fundamental characteristic of being human–to continue living. It goes against self-preservation. People normally fight for and cling to life, and suicide is premature death, a death sooner than is acceptable.

Illness: Healthy people don't die by suicide. The person would have to have a mental illness, not be in his right mind, and be full of irrational thinking. The person is sick and the causes of the sickness are treatable and preventable. Death isn't treatable, but suicide is. The illness could be stopped and the suicide doesn't have to happen. No one can explain what the illness is and why suicide happens. Until there is a good explanation for what causes people to be sick enough to kill themselves, it won't be stopped, and neither of those facts should be acceptable.

Concern for Increased Incidence: Suicide sets a bad example for others, and accepting it as a normal death would set a bad precedent. It would become contagious and would make it easier for others, especially teens, to kill themselves. Saying suicide is normal would make it become rampant in society. It will become common. If it was accepted, people might stop trying to prevent it.

Social Imperative: It is important that people live within their social settings and learn to do what is normal, acceptable and legal. Suicide is contrary to what is accepted in the American culture. It is a socially unacceptable act.

Responsibility and Blame: Students were also prone to hold others responsible for the deaths and to assign blame for suicide. In their view, suicide was a failure to act competently by, among others, the medical people, counselors, the drug companies, and the health care system. Some students also insisted that dysfunctional parenting or abusive spouses caused suicide and that it was unacceptable to cause another person to die.

Unacceptable Violence: Suicide is a kind of unnecessary violence. Accepting suicide as normal would be the same thing as accepting homicide as normal. Society should never accept any kind of violence as normal.

Numbers and Norms: Some students expressed pragmatic opposition to death by suicide, stating that statistically, self-inflicted death is uncommon. The majority of people do not kill themselves, and it would be acceptable only if the majority died by it.

Moral Concerns: These repetitious beliefs are introduced in the next chapter.

As stated above, these answers reflect familiar attitudes and beliefs that pass from one generation to the next and culturally mark suicide as a social taboo. The resulting stigma is a psychologically projected and mentally perceived mark of shame that is rooted in society's tendency to blame and hold someone accountable for suicide. Even a man putting a gun to his head can blame someone else for what he is about to do. No less than a murderer might be stigmatized for a death committed at his hands, suicide survivors sometimes sense themselves marked by the decedent's self-destructive act. The unfairness of this sensation is that the suicide survivor, unlike the murderer, has had no real hand in the death.

Stigma is closely associated with events that occur after the cause of death is apparent. Mark Solomon described events that can result in a survivor's feeling marked by suicide. These include encountering gossip, blame, social avoidance, and unpleasant public contacts. [63]

Suicide survivors are frequently aware of gossip about the death, sometimes of an insensitive nature. Some survivors are blatantly accused of responsibility for the suicide, especially when a suicide note blames the survivor for the death. The survivor might also feel avoided by friends or family. Some among the survivor's contacts might stubbornly refuse to acknowledge the suicidal nature of the death and rather talk of it as if it were an accident. A conspiracy of silence sometimes develops in which both the topic of death and the suicide are generally avoided.

Finally, suicide survivors can find contacts with officials abrasive or unsympathetic. Although reporters and broadcasters have become more sensitive about the impact of a local suicide upon survivors, all suicide survivors are affected by any suicide that is sensationalized by the media. Such experiences tend to elicit feelings of shame among survivors.

Many people look upon suicide as a shameful death. Gerald Ginsburg studied public conceptions and attitudes toward suicide in the Reno, Nevada area. A large number of people interviewed believed suicide brings shame, disgrace, guilt or responsibility for the death upon the decedent's family. Ginsburg concluded that a pall of stigma is cast over both the decedent and the survivor after a suicide, and he believed the resulting sense of social disgrace is a significant torment within suicide grief.

Not all suicide survivors experience stigma. In fact, Mark Solomon suggested that only one-third believe themselves to be stigmatized by the suicide. He also concluded that stigma is not overly troublesome among those who do encounter it. Solomon added that potentially stigmatizing events are neither necessary nor sufficient in themselves to result in stigma.

Nearly three-quarters of the survivors Solomon interviewed had encountered at least one negative event and one-third reported encountering several of them. Only 18% of the survivors experienced no stigmatizing events during their grieving. Interestingly, some survivors who experienced none of the stigmatizing events still sensed the sting of stigma. On the other hand, some survivors who experienced many negative events did not feel stigmatized by the suicide.

Solomon noted that the survivors most likely to feel stigmatized by a suicide were also those likely to have encountered many more negative events than survivors who did not feel stigmatized. This suggests stigma, if encountered at all, results not from any particular negative event, but from an accumulated effect of experiencing a number of negative experiences after a suicide.

DELIBERATE ABANDONMENT

Feeling deserted by the decedent was described as a common reaction among all survivors in Chapter Five. The sensation of being deserted seldom implies any deliberateness or intentionality on the part of the decedent, however. Therefore, it usually is not an intense or troublesome reaction to death. The grief of many other-than-natural death survivors generally includes a reaction going beyond this feeling of desertion.

Other-than-natural death survivors frequently feel deliberately abandoned by the decedent. This reaction is probably associated with the apparent preventability of these deaths. Unlike desertion, deliberate abandonment implies an "on purpose" motive on the part of the decedent. Intentionality can seem especially evident in certain circumstances, for example, when a death occurs after the survivor and decedent have had an argument, fight, or disagreement.

If the deceased walked out on the survivor during an angry argument and was killed in an automobile accident, the survivor might unconsciously believe the decedent deliberately walked out and "left" the survivor on purpose. Death feels like a purposeful leaving.

Among most other-than-natural death survivors, the feeling of deliberate abandonment loses intensity as bereavement progresses. As grief emotions subside, the circumstances of the death are viewed more realistically, and survivors can accept that the decedent did not deliberately intend to die.

The self-inflicted nature of suicide obviously makes it difficult for suicide survivors to disregard intentionality in the decedent's motives. Suicidal death is more than just a choice to die. Many times it is interpreted as the decedent's choice to leave the survivor, rather than to leave the burdens of life and illness behind. The death seems "personal." At that point, a suicide survivor confuses the decedent's intention to die with an intention on his or her part to leave the survivor, even though the two conclusions are not the same thing. Suicide survivors, then, frequently experience feeling deliberately abandoned by the deceased, and they typically have a more difficult time resolving this special grief reaction than do other non-natural death survivors.

This reaction is discussed in greater detail in the next chapter's description of rejection.

eight

No Other Survivor Could Imagine

*"I miss him in the weeping of the rain;
I want him at the shrinking of the tide."*
Edna St. Vincent Millay [64]

Grief reactions common both in suicide bereavement and in other forms of grieving have been described in the previous three chapters. The description of grief reactions experienced by suicide survivors ends in this chapter with a discussion of reactions uncommon to any other but suicide bereavement. Although these particular reactions are present in other forms of bereavement, they are rare among most survivors. Research among the survivors who have experienced an AIDS-related death of a loved one does suggest that some do encounter these reactions also. The presence of these reactions during bereavement, however, remains a strong indication that the death was suicidal.

All suicide survivors do not experience rare reactions. However, these reactions occur consistently, frequently, and often intensely enough among suicide survivors to be significant and powerful deterrents to successful resolution of grief. The existence of these rare and special reactions has led many researchers to view suicide bereavement as unique. In a sense, because they happen so infrequently among all other survivors, these reactions might well be described as unique to suicide survivorship.

As evidenced in the preceding chapters, there is more to suicide bereavement than just these rare reactions. Suicide survivorship is predominantly comprised of the complex of grief reactions "normal" in other bereavements. That being true, the grief reactions that are special and unique to suicide still account for a small, but important part of the survivor's experience.

Included among the special grief reactions that might be viewed as unique to suicide survivorship are denial of the cause of death, a sense of rejection by the decedent, embarrassment regarding the death, a fear of insanity, the death as a moral issue, and communication problems.

DENIAL OF THE CAUSE OF DEATH

Each person in our society decides what to think about the act of suicide, and most people develop a bias against it early in childhood. Young children know about suicide. They understand it is the act of killing one's self. They talk about suicide, think about it sometimes as a way to get back at parents, and sometimes threaten it when they are angry. Children also learn such an act is unacceptable, frightening, "wrong," or "bad."

During adolescence, young people frame the concept of suicide within more rigid, moralistic views. Usually, by the time a person reaches adulthood, attitudes about the "wrongness" of self-destruction are well ingrained. Suicide, then, is typically seen as distasteful, repugnant, abhorrent, sinful, selfish, hateful, or evil. The negative view of suicide is so deeply ingrained that, for most people, considering self-inflicted death as a normal or acceptable alternative to life's sufferings is terribly difficult even when in the most trying of times. In this way, negative beliefs about suicide serve as prohibitions against it.

* * *

> "No way was I going to tell anyone it was a suicide. *I* didn't believe it myself at the time."
>
> A Survivor

* * *

Suicide survivors are as likely as any other individual to have developed negative feelings toward suicide early in life. When they experience a suicide, therefore, they run headlong into their own biases against it. On a psychological level, the survivor deals with suicide, and feelings about it, in one of two ways.

First, the survivor can accept the suicidal nature of the death. This also permits him to continue to accept the decedent as a "good" person. Second, the survivor can reject suicide in some moral or negative sense. In this case, it is harder for him to accept the decedent, and the survivor often ends grief by rejecting the decedent instead. After a suicide, the survivor is challenged to separate feelings about the actions of the decedent from feelings about the decedent herself.

These two choices present the survivor with a "dilemma of resolution." Accepting the decedent is experienced as accepting suicide. Rejecting suicide is experienced as rejecting the decedent. This dilemma is especially apparent among survivors who had been involved in a close, satisfying relationship with the decedent. It is difficult to both accept the decedent and the self-inflicted death. Survivors who do not reject the decedent out-right must deal with their feelings and attitudes about suicide. This is the dilemma of resolution.

Realistically, rejecting or accepting suicide is not a simple matter. Morally rejecting suicide is a socially conditioned, ingrained tendency. The survivor discovers, however, that rejection of the decedent on some conscious level usually follows. Most suicide survivors do not reject the decedent. The struggle then becomes one of accepting the decedent on one hand, while rejecting the self-destructive act on the other.

One way a suicide survivor can solve this dilemma is to accept the decedent without dealing with the suicide. Denial of the cause of death is a common way to escape dealing with suicide. For example, a suicide survivor might insist the cause of death was something other than suicide, referring to the death as an accident, heart attack, organ failure, or even a murder.

Denial of the suicidal nature of the death is hard to maintain, unless the cause was equivocal. For one thing, denial is easily shredded by facts surrounding the death. For another, denial requires zealous effort, resulting in a heavier emotional burden for the survivor. To strengthen their defensive denial of the cause of death, survivors often stoke it with hostility and anger. Consequently, then, denial of the suicidal nature of death can lead to incomplete grieving or chronic hostility and anger.

The suicide survivor can solve the dilemma of resolution in another way, if no doubt exists about the circumstances of the death, and the survivor does not deny its cause. He does so by reframing his beliefs about suicide. The survivor makes continued acceptance of the decedent easier by viewing suicide in better than negative terms. In other words, the act is rationalized in more positive ways than it had been before the death.

Thus, suicide survivors can end the dilemma by seeing suicide as an acceptable way of dying. This does not mean these survivors think about suicide for themselves. Acceptance implies only a more open view of self-inflicted death. The survivors let go of society's judgmental views of suicide and no longer think of it as wrong, repugnant, aberrant, or sinful.

Overcoming a prejudice against suicide and accepting the death is a Herculean task. Survivors usually struggle with denial of the cause of death for some time. They waver between the ingrained rejection of suicide and the efforts to somehow accept it.

Some survivors never completely resolve this dilemma. They hold on to strictly negative attitudes toward suicide. Their acceptance of the decedent after completing the repugnant act is, therefore, marked by ambivalence, anger, and frustration. Holding on to both rejection of suicide and acceptance of the decedent requires arduous efforts.

Among survivors who had been involved in difficult, conflict-ridden, or burdensome relationships, this dilemma might not arise. If the survivor has rejected the decedent as not a worthwhile person, he can easily hold on to negative attitudes toward suicide. In fact, the very suicide supports the survivor's negative appraisal of the decedent. Consequently, the survivor rejects both the decedent and the act of suicide with little change in attitudes toward either.

* * *

"He was just the kind of person who would do *that* to his family."

A Survivor

* * *

Denial of the cause of death makes suicide survivorship different from any other bereavement from the start. No other survivors deal with the cause of death with such painful effort. No other survivors must so completely reconcile both the death itself and its cause. Such reconciliation is an important part of most suicide bereavements and, if the dilemma of resolution continues, the survivor's bereavement is often prolonged.

REJECTION

Feeling deserted and deliberately abandoned were described in previous chapters as parts of other bereavements. Among suicide survivors, sensations of this nature take on more serious and enduring proportions. In fact, beyond feeling deserted or deliberately abandoned, suicide survivors might experience the death as an outright and intentional rejection by the decedent.

Rejection might he somehow implied or inferred by a survivor in other forms of death, but be outside the awareness and thoughts of comforters. In suicide, rejection is determined by a very specific act performed by the decedent, and after the death, survivors find it difficult to define the act in any other way than as a rejection. It appears there are few suicide survivors who do not experience the death in this way for periods of time.

That suicide survivors commonly feel the decedent chose to leave them or rejected them, clearly and consistently distinguishes suicide bereavements from others. Most suicide survivors feel rejected by the decedent, while few other survivors experience any degree of personal rejection.

Charles Neuringer concluded that suicide is unique among the ways of dying because of the strong message that it carries to the survivor. [65] The suicide makes a statement about the feelings that were shared between the decedent and survivor. The conscious deliberateness of purpose in the act intensifies the survivor's impression that he was deserted because the shared feelings were inadequate.

Some survivors actually consider the death as the decedent's way to bring revenge upon them. Suicide survivors frequently feel the decedent was somehow getting even with them by dying. Although this might seem like just a "paranoid" reaction by the survivor, in some cases such feelings are valid. Karl Menninger suggested that the decedent often kills herself for the express purpose of taking revenge upon the survivor. [66] The resultant feelings of rejection and abandonment experienced by the survivor are almost always inherent in the self-destructive act itself. Potentially compounding this reaction, the sensation of being rejected is amplified in any situation in which the decedent leaves a "suicide note" that in any way blames or criticizes the survivor.

That suicide communicates a message of rejection often carries beyond the immediate relationship with the close survivor. As Robert Kastenbaum suggested, the person who completes suicide seems to flaunt society, hinting that the kind of lives we have built for ourselves are not worth keeping. The person rejects sanctions against suicide, thereby assaulting the social fabric that ties all of us together as humans. Perhaps it is this assault, this apparent indictment against our lives, that makes suicidal death so generally troublesome to most of us. Even so, the survivor remains the one who deals intimately with the rejecting aspect of suicide. Kastenbaum concluded that, more than rejecting a way of life, the decedent rejects the option to share in the love and the life offered by the survivor. It is the survivor who bears the brunt of the decedent's rejection. [67]

EMBARRASSMENT

Bereaved survivors usually do not feel embarrassed by the death of another person, unless that death happens to be a suicide. Feeling embarrassment is a rare reaction to death and is largely unique to suicide survivorship.

Suicide survivors frequently say that admitting to a suicide within the family is accompanied by shameful feelings. They feel acknowledging the suicidal nature of a death also implies something about themselves. Survivors also tend to feel other people look upon them in a less than favorable light after the suicide.

Social attitudes toward suicide are at the root of this reaction. Many people believe something is terribly wrong with anyone who completes suicide or that something is wrong somewhere in her life. The suicide survivor is as likely as anyone else to embrace this belief on a deep, psychological level. Consequently, the survivor naturally thinks others have made a judgment against the decedent.

Assuming the judgments of others based on our own internal perceptions is called "projection" in psychology. In this case, survivors project their own beliefs onto others; that is, because they believe something must have been wrong with the decedent to choose to die by suicide, they assume others will think the same thing.

Survivors who consider suicide to be evidence of insanity experience a troubling consequence of projection. This shame-filled view of suicide combined with the survivor's projection of beliefs can result in the following illogical thinking: "Anyone who completes suicide must be crazy. My _____ must have been crazy because she took her own life. If others find out she completed suicide, they'll think she was crazy." Some survivors follow this non-logic with a question. "If they think she was crazy, they'll think I'm crazy, too."

The embarrassment or shame suicide survivors feel creates more difficult social interactions than otherwise normal during grieving. Suicide survivors initially experience discomfort in revealing the cause of death. Conversations with casual acquaintances or strangers fill survivors with anxiety that the secret of the suicide might somehow come to light. Some survivors tell people the death was an accident. Others are vague when discussing the circumstances of the death. In extreme cases, suicide survivors avoid talking about the death, or even bringing up the decedent's name, altogether.

The survivor's embarrassment can lead to strained social interactions or avoidance of contact with others. Therefore, more than any other survivor, the suicide survivor might deliberately stay away from people who could be helpful in resolving the grief.

FEAR OF INSANITY

Many suicide survivors experience apprehension about losing their own sanity. This is not surprising, since most survivors are unfamiliar with the intense emotional reactions common to suicide bereavement. Feeling suddenly uprooted, untethered, or uncontrolled is extremely disquieting. Additionally, any survivor is likely to be troubled by his behavior if grief is expressed through uncharacteristic acting out of anger, hostility, or sorrow. Momentary thoughts like "I'm going crazy," "I'm losing my mind," "I can't stand another minute of this," or "I'm losing all control" are common.

Compounding an awareness that behavior and emotions seem to be beyond control, depression verging on despair can develop as the grief process progresses. The future might seem empty of any hope or promise for the survivor. Doubt that life will ever again he rewarding or satisfying grows. To the survivor, the world becomes an unsafe place in which the rug can simply be yanked from beneath her at any moment. The survivor's trust in the goodness of life vanishes.

In the face of such pervasive hopelessness and amid the fear of lost mental control, a survivor is sometimes besieged by thoughts of his own suicide. This might be the first, and only, time the survivor has ever seriously entertained vivid self-destructive thoughts. Under these traumatic developments, the survivor naturally fears he will be unable to prevent the completion of his own suicidal ideas.

Finally, a large segment of our population believes the myth that people who perform suicide are seriously mentally ill or psychologically unbalanced. While current research has found that more than 90% of those who killed themselves had one or more diagnosed mental disorders, suicide does not necessarily reflect the act of a mentally unstable or momentarily deranged individual. Fears that the decedent was "crazy" might lurk somewhere in darkened corners of the survivor's mind, even if he has been able to unearth a plausible explanation for the suicide. Any fear that the decedent really was "crazy" can be twisted into a similar fear that the survivor is a little insane, also. Fears like these feed upon underlying anxieties that suicidal behavior is contagious or runs in families, and they are heightened by the survivor's own suicidal thoughts.

* * *

"If it's all genetics, then I'm no different than him, am I?"

A Survivor

* * *

Understandably, fears and anxieties about the survivor's own mental and psychological stability become an addition to the burden of suicide bereavement.

THE DEATH AS A MORAL ISSUE

Bible scriptures do not specifically address suicide, nor pronounce a judgment upon it. The moral injunction against suicide has not been passed by the lips of God, but by the condemning voices of men inferring, assuming, or perhaps presuming, to know the mind of God on this matter.

St. Augustine (354-430 C.E.) was alarmed by the number of Christians who zealously sought eternal glory by actively courting or bringing about their own deaths; they were the noble martyrs of their era. Augustine spoke out against suicide in his comments to the Church, exhorting the end of self-inflicted death. The Church finally responded in 533 C.E., defining suicide as the deadliest of mortal sins.

Labeling an unacceptable act a sin might increase the guilt associated with performance of that act, but it has never fully deterred people from indulging in the "sinful" act. Therefore, labeling suicide a sin has never been the deterrent Augustine might have hoped it would be. The label has, however, added significantly to the suicide survivor's burden in resolving grief.

The many points offered by university students to support their view that suicide was not normal and should not be accepted included religious and moral aspects. Self-inflicted death clearly goes against many students' religious tenets, and they believe strongly that suicide is a sin and against God's will. Some stated that it is against God's plan for each life. Other students said that suicide is being ungrateful for the life given by God, and that life should be cherished. For these students, suicide is a death difficult to forgive.

Without framing their opposition in religious terms, a fair number of students expressed a moral perspective in a more general sense. For them, suicide is against a code of life. It is just wrong, and, if it was normal, people wouldn't feel guilty about doing it or about surviving after someone else does it.

Most of the legal statutes declaring suicide a crime have been removed from active law or have long been ignored. Those who attempt suicide are seldom legally degraded, fined, or prosecuted. Yet, students will periodically maintain that suicide is illegal in support of their view that it is an unacceptable form of death.

Unfortunately for survivors after a suicide, the attitudes and religious injunctions against self-inflicted death remain. Many Churches, although more sensitive to the trauma of survivors, have not revised their position on the sinfulness of suicide. The Church's traditional opinion on self-inflicted murder was that the victim had no opportunity to atone for the act, thereby negating any chance of God's forgiveness. The victim surrendered her life and condemned her soul to damnation.

Only suicide survivors deal with moral considerations of the cause of death. They worry about the state of the decedent's soul and often seek reassurance from clergy members that the decedent has not been damned to hell. This reassurance is difficult to obtain, not because the clergy is unsympathetic, but because survivors are so aware of the Church's traditional stance on suicide. They do not find it easy to forget the "deadliest of mortal sins."

Moral and religious concerns are hard to resolve. For survivors who consider suicide in a strictly moral sense, absolution and forgiveness can be extended to the decedent more easily than the survivors who wrestle with their own religious beliefs about taking a life. For them, real answers are nonexistent, at least in this life. Many survivors carry their worries for the decedent's soul with them for the rest of their own lives. Others choose to rely on God's mercy and benevolence and, thereby, let go of this particular worry.

COMMUNICATION PROBLEMS

A realistic and honest acceptance of circumstances surrounding a death is the foundation of healthy grieving. Additionally, successful completion of any bereavement is influenced by the opportunity for the survivor to talk openly and honestly about grief. When a survivor is not able to be honest about the circumstances surrounding the death, grieving is inhibited.

Only among suicide survivors are communication difficulties regarding the death common. Emotional grief reactions, like denial, shame, guilt, and stigma, typical in suicide bereavement, make dealing with the suicide hard and hinder the survivor's communication of grief.

For example, denial that the death was a suicide can be so strong that the survivor vehemently and, many times, violently confronts anyone daring to suggest the death was self-inflicted. Open hostility like this sometimes extends even to those attempting just to talk about the death.

Some survivors insist the death was accidental, even when obvious evidence betrays the suicide, like when a note reveals self-intended death. Depending on the vehemence of the survivor's denial, the discomfort of people intending to console the survivor increases. Already without socially approved and "proper" condolences to extend to the suicide survivor, the comforter can be further confused at encountering hostility. Both survivor and comforter find openly expressing themselves difficult, and each might seek to avoid the other, alienating the survivor further.

Some survivors, shamed beyond tolerance, distort or deliberately conceal the truth about the death. This happens especially in families with surviving young children. Sometimes adults insist the cause of death was natural, even when the child is aware of the self-destructive act, as would be the case if the child witnessed the death or discovered the body. Adults often do not allow children to talk about the death or demand they keep its cause a secret from others.

Children are confused by such experiences. They learn that talking about death is to be avoided, or that, if it is talked about, it is not done so in frank or honest terms. Children also learn from this to distrust their own perceptions of reality and to doubt the assertions of important people around them.

An excellent example of disruption of open communication is often observed among fathers of adolescent suicides. Some fathers display outrage and hostility toward anyone wanting to talk about the death. They sometimes adamantly insist the death was an accident and rage if the death certificate is signed as a suicide. In extreme cases, some parents resolutely declare the death to have been a murder and identify the person they believe killed their teenager. The difficulties these parents have in dealing with suicide are worthy of understanding and sympathy. A young person's suicide seems particularly troubling and abhorrent. In fact, Pamela Cantor suggested that grief reactions common within suicide bereavement might actually be further accentuated with the suicide of a young person. [68]

The inability to talk openly and honestly about suicide is common throughout our society. The difficulty this presents to survivors can have enduring effects. If survivors cannot find a forum in which to discuss the suicide, communication problems intensify and grief stalls.

What chance is there for recovery from grief?

This chapter concludes the description of the predominant grief reactions regularly experienced by suicide survivors. It is apparent that bereavement marked by so many reactions leaves the survivor in a vulnerable position and that the complex interaction of any number of such intense reactions often results in a difficult grief experience for the survivor. The ways suicide survivors manage their bereavement and the expected grief outcomes after a suicide are the topics of the next chapters.

nine

The Aftermath

"We who have come back, we know: the best of us did not return."
Victor E. Frankl [69]

Any survivor would be comforted by the assurance that complete recovery from grief and reconstruction of a satisfying life will be accomplished by two years after the death. Grief is too inconsistent in expression among individuals to be predictable in course, however. Projecting ahead is impossible.

Survivors grieve in different ways. The manner in which one person might experience grief is determined by the interaction of various factors. Among the most important of these factors, John McIntosh included: the family relationship between survivor and deceased, the survivor's social support network, individual personality and coping abilities, emotional attachment or closeness to the deceased, and the ages of both survivor and deceased. [70]

Factors That Influence Grief

The type and quality of relationship lost by the survivor dramatically influence the severity of grief. Bereavements differ among survivors who are spouses, parents, children, brothers, sisters, uncles, friends, lovers, work associates, or casual acquaintances of the decedent. The quality of the relationship, whether it was pleasant, hostile, shallow, intense, satisfying, painful, growing, or deteriorating at the time of death, further affects the experience of grief. For example, a wife who enjoyed a pleasant, growing, and maturing relationship with the decedent experiences a grief different from a wife who had a painful, destructive, and deteriorating relationship.

Personal characteristics of the survivor also affect bereavement. These include: age, personality features, life experiences, prior grief experiences, faith, attitudes, beliefs, and reality perceptions. Generally, then, a survivor's personal attributes partly determine intensity and duration of grief reactions.

Personality development continues throughout an individual's life and reflects his life-long experiences. The foundations of personality, however, are laid down in childhood and adolescence, long before involvement in adult relationships. Among adult survivors, therefore, reactions to death will mirror individualistic and characteristic responses typical of the survivor in past stressful situations. For example, a person might characteristically become hyperactive and anxious when under stress.

Primary responses to stress developed early in life are likely to be predominant during bereavement. They also tend to overshadow other grief reactions. Thus, a survivor's activity and anxiety might be obvious, while his guilt, fear, loneliness, and preoccupation with the deceased are little noticed. Unfortunately, little regarded grief reactions become little resolved reactions.

Circumstances surrounding the death are clearly significant in determining the course of bereavement. As explained in previous chapters, the survivor's reactions to the death are influenced by whether the death was of natural or other-than-natural cause, whether it was expected or came suddenly, and whether it was unintentional or deliberate. Additional grief reactions are consistently associated to deaths that are not expected or by natural cause. In fact, the more troublesome the circumstances of the death for the survivor, the greater will be the number and intensity of grief reactions.

Finally, circumstances after a death contribute to the bereavement process. Life in the aftermath of death is different for each survivor. For example, among survivors who lose a marital partner, financial stability and security vary. Some have to return immediately to work, change jobs, or find work for the first time, whereas others remain at home, quit jobs, or take extended leaves of absence. If the survivors are parents, they might find the level of conflict elevated in their own marriage, or the death might bring them into a closer relationship with each other. Some survivors initiate a move to a new residence or locality (itself a major stressor) and others stay entrenched where they had been before the death.

The circumstances into which a survivor is thrust after a death not only have important effects upon bereavement, they also highlight another fact. After a death, survivors quickly discover life does not halt while the grief work goes along. In fact, the pace of life often accelerates in many ways.

Survivors learn that channeling emotional energy exclusively into grieving is not possible. At times, grief must be set aside while survivors attend to changes in their lives. Most survivors are gradually able to refocus their energies away from grieving for longer periods. Fortunately in this regard, the distress of grief does not continue unabated until it is finished.

Survivors are not always bundles of raw, exposed nerve endings. Even in the worst of the grieving, survivors are blessed with calm moments when the intense and overwhelming "grief pangs" are dulled.

Thus, depending upon circumstances after the death, grief usually shares time and focus with concerns for children, family, finances, jobs, school, careers, and with moments of calm, peace, and genuine laughter.

How Long Does Grief Last?

Successful resolution of grief depends upon how honestly the survivor acknowledges grief reactions and how diligently he works through them. The survivor must expend time and effort in doing so. Frequently and understandably, survivors wonder how long their grief will continue.

We should be cautious about assigning specific time limits to bereavement. Studies of grief indicate that grief's duration varies from one survivor to the next, depending on many of the factors just discussed. Some survivors perform the grief work relatively quickly, apparently completing the grief process within six months of the death. In contrast, other survivors grieve for the remainder of their lives. Generally, however, survivors complete the grief work over a period of several years.

Despite such variabilities, enough commonalities exist among survivors to permit some generalizations about how long grief endures. For instance, few survivors finish their grief within the first year after the death. Grief typically progresses through two to four years.

The intensity of principle grief reactions usually declines significantly between the first and second years of bereavement. Grief is not completed at this point, however. Survivors continue to feel some degree of loneliness, psychological discomfort, social isolation, and impaired physical health. Survivors also tend to view the world as an insecure, hostile, and unsafe place during this time.

Grief is largely resolved by the fourth year of bereavement and, although some elements of grief linger, survivors are usually well into recovery by that time. Some survivors have brief moments of crying, longing, loneliness, or sorrow over the loss as many as six to ten years after the death. In fact, grief might never be completely finished. Many survivors periodically encounter its traces long years after the death.

The two tasks of grief have been described as emotional separation from the decedent and satisfying reconstruction of life apart from the decedent. The first task of separation is seldom accomplished significantly during grief's first year. By the end of the second year, however, most survivors have worked through the desire to hold on to, or get back, the decedent and are able to fully accept the reality of the death. This progress is marked by the survivor's willingness to see both the pleasant and unpleasant aspects of the lost relationship.

Although survivors begin rebuilding their lives early in bereavement, only after emotional detachment from the decedent is accomplished can the task of recovery from grief be earnestly pursued. The period of bereavement in which this task progresses is often called re-involvement, attachment, adjustment, recovery, or reconstruction. It seems typically to take place between the second and fourth years following the death.

During recovery the survivor's pangs of grief come in waves and are less frequent and less intense. Grief efforts focus predominantly on rebuilding a life in which the decedent is not an important living part. Survivors often move to a new locale, seek educational opportunities, start a new career, or enter new relationships during this time. Social ties are usually expanded, and hobbies or interests might be entertained with renewed zeal and satisfaction. Many survivors involve themselves in volunteer and foundation-building pursuits associated to the decedent's cause of death.

As recovery progresses, the survivor's sense of self is strengthened and self-esteem increases. A new self-confidence often develops if the survivor stretches the limits of perhaps previously untried skills and abilities. New attitudes toward life are formed.

Eventually, the survivor experiences hope that life without the decedent can be fulfilling and satisfying: that there is, after all, a glowing life at the end of the tunnel of grief.

Full recovery from a significant loss is marked by absence of intense grief reactions, by achievement of emotional stability, by re-entry into socially satisfying relationships, by finding meaning and purpose in life, and by diminished need for outside or professional support. Recovery seems most likely between the ends of the second and fourth years of grieving, although some survivors continue to struggle toward it four to six years after the death.

Within three to four years of grieving, the majority of survivors are happily reengaged in life. They find life satisfying and at least as rich and fulfilling as it was prior to the death. Many survivors even feel stronger and more competent than they did before the grief experience, viewing their struggle toward recovery as a meaningful accomplishment that they did not think they would ever be able to reach.

No matter how long recovery requires, survivors do not simply pass through their bereavement and leave it behind. Nor do they return fully to their former selves. They are not the individuals they were before the death. After surviving death and bereavement, survivors are at once somehow the same and somehow different. Though their lives can again be tasted, enjoyed, and savored in characteristic style, they will always experience a dash of loneliness, of sadness, and of yearning flavoring their lives.

Falling Short of Recovery

Recovery from grief, though always hoped for, is not always ensured. Grief can be stalled, hindered, aborted, obstructed, diverted, or interrupted before one or both of its tasks are completed. Some survivors do not successfully finish the grief work. Instead, they become casualties, or even fatalities, of the process meant to help them suffer a death and emerge from bereavement alive.

Successful grieving results in the survivor's emancipation from emotional bondage to the decedent, readjustment to a life in which the decedent is missing, and formation of new relationships. When grief does not follow its expected course, these results are not achieved. In such cases, the survivor's experience might variously he called atypical grief, delayed grief, morbid grief, pathological grief, or abnormal grief. These are all labels for essentially the same thing, that is, a grief that has not ended in recovery.

What prevents some survivors from completing the grief work? Erich Lindemann suggested that the common obstacles to successful grieving are a survivor's attempt to avoid the intense distress connected with grief or to avoid the expression of emotion necessary to exhaust it. The tendency to avoid the entire complex of grief reactions at any cost is indicated in various behaviors, like a survivor's refusing visits from others to avoid talking about the death. [71]

Lindemann referred to the reactions that subvert grieving, or that distort natural reactions, to be morbid or abnormal grief reactions. He suggested that grief becomes abnormal, or nonfunctional, when such reactions are present. Grief reactions falling outside the realm of "normal" reactions generally arise because of delay or distortion of the normal grief reactions.

Delay of grieving is a particularly striking, and perhaps frequent, reaction to loss. Postponement of grief can have dire consequences for the survivor, as exemplified in experiences of individuals suffering delayed effects of trauma. Observations of war combat veterans experiencing symptoms of post traumatic stress disorder (ptsd) make increasingly evident the fact that delaying grief work can have enduring, disastrous, and catastrophic impact.

Grief might be put off, but it does not go away. Delayed grief continues to fester like a concealed psychic ulcer. The longer resolution of grief is delayed, the more insidious become the sores. Years after grief has normally run its course, survivors who have blocked its expression continue to use emotional energy to deal with unfinished grief reactions.

Abnormal grieving is also indicated by distorted reactions. Lindemann described several common distortions that are signs of unresolved grief. Distorted grief reactions include:

1) Patterns of overactivity in which the survivor acts as if a significant loss has not been experienced.

2) Symptoms, illness, or behaviors once displayed by the decedent: development of any form of stress-related, psychosomatic illnesses.

3) Obvious changes in relationships with friends and relatives, like chronic irritability, avoidance of former social activities, progressive social isolation, expressed desire to be left alone, or disabling fear of antagonizing others. Overflowing hostility that spreads throughout all relationships or is furiously targeted against specific people is also an example.

4) Concealment of anger and hostility at the expense of becoming wooden and formal, demonstrated in a mask-like facial expression and an absence of emotional display.

5) Lasting loss of social interaction patterns indicated by inability to initiate any activity, restlessness or sleeplessness, lack of decisiveness, or loss of promise in anything other than routine, ordinary activities carried on with little enthusiasm.

6) Involvement in activities somehow detrimental to the survivor's social or economic welfare; loss of friends because of inappropriate behavior: self-punitive behavior, like alcohol or drug abuse, compulsive spending, or gambling, with no awareness of excessive guilt; inappropriate generosity, frivolous spending, or foolish financial dealings.

7) Agitated depression with elements of tension, insomnia, feelings of worthlessness, bitter self-accusation, or obvious desire for punishment.

Delays and distortions of reactions are normal among grieving survivors. Grief work starts and stops, bores full speed ahead and sluggishly plods along, is acknowledged and denied, indulged and avoided. Most survivors eventually accomplish the work, even if some take years longer than others.

However, when the delays or distortions are excessive, inadequate or incomplete resolution of grief is probable. Survivors who forestall grief work by delaying and distorting reactions suffer the saddest outcomes of survivorship. Stuck in their grief, blocking its necessary course, they hold on to elements of grief without awareness. They do not separate from the memory of the decedent or recover from the loss.

The number of survivors who do not successfully complete the grief work and remain troubled by the death years later may constitute a substantial minority. As many as one quarter (25%) of those experiencing grief are estimated to need some sort of professional assistance at one time or another during their bereavement. Therefore, many survivors commonly and appropriately seek grief counseling.

Some, but not the majority, of suicide survivors get "stuck" in their grief, blocked by reactions typical to suicide bereavement. Obstructions to their grief can take the shape of unresolved denial, shame, concealing the nature of the death, stigmatization, blame, and accusations or assumptions regarding responsibility for the death. These grief reactions are often at odds, one with another, and their expression can present the survivor a psychological dilemma.

Expression of one natural reaction sometimes conflicts with the expression of another equally natural reaction. For example, feeling anger toward the decedent is natural during grief, but its expression often increases the survivor's guilt. On the other hand, feeling guilt is also natural, yet its expression not only can block anger, it might also generate more anger. Essentially, then, the survivor is caught between contradictory emotional reactions, each an effective psychological expression of deeply experienced pain, yet at the same time, generating equally intolerable states of distress.

Suicide survivors are susceptible to finding themselves between this psychological "rock and hard place." More opportunities for psychological dilemmas result from the greater number of grief reactions natural to suicide bereavement. For example, greater intensity of guilt might seriously hold back the expression of anger. Excessive rage directed toward the decedent increases already troubling guilt. Similarly, searching for an acceptable explanation for the suicide conflicts with the need to separate, or detach, from the decedent, while the need to separate presses the survivor to get on with things before an acceptable answer has been discovered. The need for social contact can he blocked by shame or blame, and the cry for help might be muffled by avoidance of those who would respond to it.

Severe complications of grieving commonly result in incomplete or inadequate recovery and readjustment to life. Certainly, some suicide survivors do not fair well in grieving or recovery. These survivors often continue to deny the suicidal nature of the death many years later. They also fail to engage in comfortable social interactions for a long time after the death. Kjell Rudestam believed suicide survivors who discover the decedent's body, who rationalize the suicide as a courageous or heroic act, who feel somehow stigmatized by the suicide, or who conceal the truth of the suicidal death from others are the ones most likely to find readjustment difficult after the death. [72]

Complications in grieving and recovery after suicide result from the same basic obstructions encountered in other bereavements: not because the death was suicide, but because the survivor is unable to resolve grief reactions, to separate emotionally from the decedent, and to readjust to a life in which the decedent is missing. Manifestations of unresolved grief are the same among suicide survivors as those described by Lindemann in regard to "normal" grief.

All survivors are susceptible to experiencing complications of grieving and difficulties in recovery. Such experiences are not unique to suicide bereavement. Additionally, grief complications and inadequate recovery are not universal among suicide survivors. In fact, the majority of suicide survivors show levels of recovery no different from any other survivor. Most need professional counseling no more often during bereavement than others, they are just as likely to discover purpose and satisfaction in life after bereavement, to view their current lives as better than before in many ways, to establish financial and employment stability, and to become involved in new intimate and satisfying relationships.

Recovery appears especially likely after suicide when the relationship between the survivor and decedent was positive and minimally disruptive, when the survivor is successful in placing responsibility for cause of the suicide to factors outside of his control, and in some cases, when the decedent had somehow been a burden to the survivor prior to the death.

Though they might experience a greater number and intensity of grief reactions than others, suicide survivors do not require significantly more time to accomplish the grief work. Their recovery is usually well underway between the end of the second and fourth years following the death, and is firmly established no later than between the fourth and sixth years.

What Is So Different About Suicide Survivorship?

Death, regardless of cause, is an excruciating and painful event in a survivor's life, bringing emotional, psychological, and physical upheaval. The grief that follows is stressful and burdensome. For most survivors, the devastating intensity of bereavement will not be surpassed by any other event in their lives.

Since nearly all bereavements are traumatic in some ways, there seems little reason or utility in comparing the severity of one with another. While acknowledging this, it is safe to say, because so many grief reactions are common to suicide, that no bereavement could ever be more intense or severe than suicide bereavement.

Suicide bereavement *is* different. It is different because death by suicide is different. Suicide is more than death of a loved person. Additionally, it is death experienced suddenly and unexpectedly. It is death not by natural cause. Finally, it is death unquestionably deliberate, intentional, and self-inflicted.

As described in the previous four chapters, specific grief reactions result from each of these factors. Consequently, suicide bereavement is comprised of many grief reactions, including reactions common to all losses, reactions resulting from sudden and unexpected death, reactions resulting from other-than-natural death, and reactions largely unique to suicidal death. Suicide bereavement is different because it is comprised of such varied grief reactions, some of them seldom experienced by other survivors.

Grief reactions not experienced in "normal" bereavement are frequently described as exaggerations or distorted caricatures of "normal" grief features. They are called atypical, morbid, or abnormal grief reactions. Grief reactions following a suicide tend to be more intense, longer enduring, and of greater variety. That they are beyond normal reactions leads some people to consider suicide bereavement atypical, morbid, or abnormal. Such conclusions are grave misconceptions.

That two forms of bereavement have common elements does not necessarily nor logically mean one is derived from the other, atypical or not. Suicide bereavement is not "normal" bereavement gone haywire. Suicide is death culturally considered abnormal. The belief a death is abnormal generally leads to the assumption that reactions to it are also abnormal. However, suicide grief reactions are not abnormal derivatives of normal grief. They are natural reactions to a death that is different.

Suicide survivorship is comprised, in part, of intense "normal" reactions to a significant loss and, in part, of special reactions derived from the sudden, other-than-natural, and self-inflicted nature of the death. The suicide grief process is a complex interaction of all these reactions. It is a "normal" or natural consequence to a form of death socially judged abnormal and unacceptable.

Emphasizing this point, the experience of special grief reactions common in suicide grief does not mean this bereavement is complicated, atypical, morbid, or abnormal. Bereavement after suicide is not, in any sense, abnormal. The reactions described in previous chapters are natural reactions to the special features of suicidal death. Suicide bereavement is different than other bereavements, but natural all the same.

Ultimately, comparing grief experiences of suicide survivors with those of others might be unproductive. Although suicide bereavement is primarily a normal response to a significant loss, it is also something more. Suicide bereavement is different from other bereavements, with good reason. Some elements of suicidal death are unique. Some elements of societal reactions to the death are unique. Finally, some elements of the suicide grief process are unique.

The combination of these unique elements almost demands that the final outcome of bereavement will be different for the suicide survivor. The death and its processing are different. So too, then, should be its resolution. Fortunately, and encouragingly, for suicide survivors, the differences inherent in suicide bereavement do not mean survivors suffer atypical or abnormal recovery from grief. On the contrary, most suicide survivors do as well in long-term recovery as do other survivors.

Grief's Combat Veterans

To better understand suicide bereavement, it is helpful to consider it in terms of another familiar experience in our society: that is, the experience of war's combat veterans.

Stresses, tragedies, and hardships exist for all people in the military during war periods. Commonalities of experience are based upon being anywhere in the service during a war. While these similar features comprise a large part of wartime experience, the reactions to the war, the resolution of psychological conflicts resulting from it, and the aftermath when it ends are qualitatively and quantitatively different for veterans who engaged the enemy first hand in combat compared with veterans who served in the rear areas of the combat theater or those who remained stateside and did not serve outside the country.

More succinctly, there are important differences between war experiences of combat veterans and those of noncombatant veterans. The differences make it impossible for noncombatants to fully appreciate, comprehend, or identify with the experience of combatants. Their experiences are not the same.

One Marine Corps infantryman who had fought with the 1st Marine Division on Okinawa in the last major battle of WWII when he was 19-years-old described this reality. "But no one really understands [what it's like to kill in combat and watch your buddies fall around you] unless they had a part in that action. And if you did, it's something you can't forget." [73] Another Marine who had fought in a series of battles in the Republic of Vietnam when he was 19-years-old and was wounded seriously enough to be evacuated from the jungles, agrees. "Combat does not leave the mind, it stays forever." [74] The WWII combat veteran has carried the memories of those events for sixty-eight years, the Vietnam veteran for forty-seven years.

It is clear that war's combat veterans, after facing uncertain death and inflicting harm upon others, encounter difficulties in readjusting to peace that other veterans do not. A minor percentage of returning combat veterans fails at this readjustment and become post facto casualties, even fatalities, of the war experience. Some rear echelon and stateside veterans also fail to successfully readjust to peacetime life; so this experience is not unique to the minority of combat veterans. Most veterans, however, including combat veterans, make these adjustments and reenter civilian life adequately.

It is also important to note severe complications and difficulties in readjustment are not universal among all combat veterans. Their war experience might be more intense, stressful, and traumatic than other veterans, but the majority of combat veterans do not encounter overwhelming obstacles in recovering from the war or in readjusting to peace. The combat veterans will, however, be forever different because of their experiences.

Post traumatic stress disorder among Vietnam's combat veterans was long sensationalized in the media. However, research has shown that the vast majority of America's combat veterans from Vietnam, even those who have dealt with post traumatic stress, adjusted adequately in the aftermath of their traumatic war experiences. Most went on to live productive, purposeful, and satisfying lives.

Comparison of the relationship of suicide survivorship to other bereavements can be made to the relationship between combat experiences and non-combat experiences. The grief process following the death of a loved one is war. Survivors are the veterans. Suicide survivors are the combat veterans. Survivors of unexpected and other-than-natural death besides suicide are the rear area noncombatants. The survivors of expected natural death are the stateside noncombatants.

While similar features are found in the experiences of all survivors and all veterans, special and significant differences exist among suicide survivors and combatants. In no way does this suggest bereavements resulting from non-suicidal death are not traumatic experiences. Death is a tragic event for all concerned. The resultant grief process, like war, is stressful for all who live through it. For suicide survivors, like combatants, the experience is different.

Just as it is true that a few survivors of other bereavements do not successfully finish their grieving, it is also true that a majority of suicide survivors do find hope, purpose, and reward in the completion of their grief work.

The analogy drawn between suicide survivors and combat veterans emphasizes a point often missed by those who do not understand bereavement following suicide. As individuals engaged in the serious business of suicide bereavement, suicide survivors forever leave behind cherished parts of themselves: parts like innocence, simple trust, naivety, spontaneity, a view of the world as a safe place, and the freedom to love easily. They emerge from their experience transformed, possessing different views and attitudes toward life than they had before the suicide. They, the combatants, experience an event and a grief process other survivors cannot fully appreciate or comprehend. Their transformation in the war zone of suicide bereavement makes them forever different.

Although made different by their experiences, suicide survivors do get on with their lives. They *do* recover admirably, finding meaning and satisfaction in lives forever changed.

ten

Surviving Suicide Bereavement

"No suicide dies alone. His exodus from life hurts everyone around him."
William L. Coleman [75]

Grieving is an extremely disruptive experience in a person's life regardless of cause of death. Physical, emotional, and psychological stresses are amplified. Behaviors and habit patterns are disturbed. Relationships with others are strained and often severed. The risks of illness, accidents, and death are increased. In sum, grief can be a dangerous and possibly life-threatening experience.

How do people survive grieving and get on with their lives? Survivors take any of several avenues for getting through their grief. Some count on the support of family and friends. Others do it alone, isolating themselves and keeping their grief private. Many survivors seek professional help to deal with grief.

Individuals grieve in their own ways. Those who do rebuild their lives credit various factors important in their recoveries. One factor, in particular, is mentioned consistently in the stories of survivors who master grief. It is the opportunity to talk openly, freely, and often at great length about their grief.

Talking about grieving is important, probably essential, to the resolution of grief. When asked to look back upon the years of their bereavement, many survivors wonder if some early counseling would have made their grieving more bearable. Even those who were surrounded by supportive friends and family believed an objective perspective from someone with an understanding of grief would have eased some of the more troubling aspects of bereavement, the features that survivors often find themselves trying to figure out alone.

People are frequently at a loss when it comes to consoling, comforting, supporting, or nurturing the survivor. Survivors find themselves at times without anyone who understands the troubling reactions they face. For this reason, it is common for survivors to seek the professional help of a minister, doctor, counselor, psychologist, or psychiatrist.

Cause of death does not seem to affect the decision to enter counseling. As many as 75% of all adult survivors might try professional counseling at least once after the death. Nearly 65% will return for counseling more than once.

Although suicide survivors face a complex array of grief reactions like those described in earlier chapters, they are able to successfully recover from grief as well as other survivors. Additionally, they appear to accomplish their grieving in much the same manner as others and do so in similar periods of time.

How Suicide Survivors Grieve

Suicide survivors work through grief in familiar ways. Many are fortunate enough to have understanding and supportive family and friends in whom they confide. Some grieve alone, dealing with the many grief reactions as best they can and managing, with time, to put their lives back together. Suicide survivors engage in professional counseling in numbers similar to other survivors. In fact, 65% of adult suicide survivors seek counseling at least once, and 64% return for counseling more than once.

As in other bereavements, a few suicide survivors come to terms with the nature of the death, accept the death, and re-engage in a satisfying life relatively quickly. This occurs within the first year following the death in some cases. Most suicide survivors work more slowly than this through the grief process, moving gradually, resolutely, and often deliberately toward the resolution of their grief. Among these survivors, separation from intense attachment to the deceased has usually been accomplished well before the fourth year. Also, by the end of the fourth year, re-involvement in life has typically progressed to the point the survivor believes life has meaning, is worth living, is satisfying, and is better in some ways than before the death.

Finally, like other bereavements, a few suicide survivors continue to struggle with their grief as long as six years after the death. Life continues to be terribly disrupted and painful for these survivors. Time does not bring healing. For these survivors, professional help might he a necessary catalyst for resolving personal and grief issues.

Help With The Healing

Suicide survivors are a special group of people, made so by the various aspects of suicide bereavement. Relationships between professionals and suicide survivors also have special aspects. In 1973, Edwin Shneidman coined the term postvention for special efforts directed toward suicide survivors. [76] He described postvention as activities that reduce the after-effects of a traumatic event. [77] These activities help survivors live longer, more productive, and less stressful lives than they might do otherwise. The goal of postvention is to help suicide survivors deal with emotional and psychological reactions to the death.

Shneidman maintained that postvention adds a measure of stability in the survivor's life, providing interpersonal relationships in which honest feelings need not be suppressed or dissembled. Ideally, postvention provides the survivor an arena to express normally guarded emotions that might not otherwise be aired. The survivor freely vents "negative" emotions like anger, guilt, envy, shame, and irritation. Shneidman added that most survivors are willing or eager to talk with others about their grief, especially to professionally-oriented persons.

Postvention efforts are important in the initial period of shock following the suicide and in the more enduring day-to-day living with grief that continues beyond the first year of bereavement. Contact must be established between survivor and professional for postvention efforts to be undertaken, and involved professionals recommend that postvention efforts should begin as soon after the death as possible, particularly within the first 24 to 72 hours.

Survivors seldom initiate this contact early in bereavement. Considering the overwhelming complex of reactions occurring early in grief, it is not surprising that a rational decision to seek professional help is beyond the emotional and psychological inclinations of most survivors. Additionally, Lee Ann Hoff believed another reason suicide survivors get such little early help is that most suicides do not occur among people who have received prior counseling help and, therefore, the survivors are not likely to consider it for themselves early in their grief. [78]

Since suicide survivors are little inclined to seek professional help early when it would be quite advantageous, Edwin Shneidman, Lee Ann Hoff and others have maintained that an active out-reach program for suicide survivors is an ideal way to initiate postvention efforts.

Out-reach is a basic component of any comprehensive community crisis service.

Crisis Centers and Suicide Prevention Centers across the United States have developed postventive out-reach programs. Donna Junghardt described such a suicide survivor follow-up program established in the 1970s by the San Bernadino County Department of Public Health in California for the purpose of bringing support and comfort to family survivors. The out-reach program established contact with survivors 24 to 48 hours after the death and before the funeral, when possible. This particular postvention program proceeded through three phases. [79]

Phase one begins with the initial contact of the survivor. The goals of this phase are to help the survivor withstand the initial shock of immense loss and to increase his or her understanding of basic grief emotions. Facing the reality and facts about the suicide are not critical during this initial phase.

Phase two takes place during the six months after the funeral. Regular meeting times are set up with either individual family members or with a group. In the first week after the funeral two or three meetings are sometimes necessary. Afterwards, weekly meetings are typically adequate for about three or four weeks. The initial crisis period is usually passed after the sixth week, and meetings are then scheduled at two or three week intervals. The goals of these meetings are to facilitate reintegration of the family, to help the survivor deal with the grief process, to help her understand the dynamics of grieving, and to deal with whatever emotions, social problems, or crises arise.

Phase three begins after the six-month anniversary of the suicide. At this point renewal and rejuvenation begin to take place and little need for professional contact exists. The survivors are revisited around the suicide's first year anniversary to see how well the family is doing and to determine if any problems have developed that might require more therapeutic contact.

Today, one organization that started on the East Coast in 1987 stands out in its suicide prevention, postvention, and out-reach efforts on behalf of survivors. The American Foundation for Suicide Prevention (AFSP) was started by a group of individuals who had experienced the suicide of a loved one, and it has grown into a nationwide organization with more than fifty local chapters. The mission of the AFSP was to support suicide research and education and to develop effective suicide prevention efforts. In addition to the goals of better understanding and preventing suicide, the founders also recognized the importance of helping the bereaved survivors cope with the death and find the support they need. [80]

Since being established, the AFSP has "mobilized and connected tens of thousands of people who have lost a family member, loved one, or friend to suicide," giving survivors a forum to honor their loved ones "and remember them by how they lived, not only how they died." The foundation provides opportunities for survivors to volunteer and "to get involved in ways that make sense to them," offering a variety of resources and programs to meet its goals. Survivors can deliver prevention programs to schools and businesses, reach out to survivors of suicide loss, organize fundraising events, volunteer as public speakers, and act as an available resource for their home communities. They also participate in training programs to become volunteer facilitators for grief support groups.

Several annual events have placed the AFSP at the forefront of increasing public awareness of suicide risk and the possibility of preventing self-inflicted deaths. Thousands of people join nationwide to participate in community *Out of the Darkness* Walks. Organized on a local level, the walks raise money for research and education programs and bring messages to the communities about depression and suicide.

Perhaps more importantly, the walks connect survivors and families to others who have lost someone to suicide, providing all who participate a measure of comfort and support. Additionally, since 1998, on one Saturday in mid-November, *International Survivors of Suicide Day*, a panel of suicide survivors and mental health professionals discuss the impact of suicide and the grief process in a special 90-minute-broadcast that is viewed around the world.

In the twenty-six years since it was first organized, the American Foundation for Suicide Prevention has remained a vital beacon of hope to survivors and communities. Through its website, social media, brochures, and press releases the AFSP has provided information to hundreds of thousands of people.

The out-reach concept is effective for suicide survivors because, as suggested above, so few survivors perceive a need to contact a professional during the early period of emotional and psychological shock following the death. Few survivors look for this contact during the first year of bereavement when it would be most helpful, although many survivors say they would have welcomed the offer of help from a trained professional at the time of the suicide.

Out-reach programs are beneficial, but they are difficult to conduct, primarily because suicide survivors are hard to identify from among other survivors. Cause of death in the case of suicide is not reported in obituaries, unless a family chooses to make the cause of death public. Also, confidentiality issues restrict access to death certificates and prohibit dissemination of information by funeral directors. Therefore, beyond their own media advertising of available services, out-reach volunteers often rely on "word-of-mouth notification" and then find ways to engage contact with the survivors.

The comforters and out-reach volunteers are in better positions to shoulder the responsibility of initiating postvention efforts, rather than leaving it up to the individuals least able to do so: that is, the suicide survivors themselves. Yet, the negative social beliefs and attitudes that darkly color suicide remain the challenge to connecting survivors and out-reach volunteers. As long as suicide is shrouded in stigma, myth, and taboo, out-reach programs offering service to its survivors will be deterred from establishing life-giving contacts.

Suicide Survivors' Support Groups

Instead of individual counseling, suicide survivors quite frequently look for support in one group or another for help in grieving. Most adult survivors are aware of several types of support groups available in their communities: for example, survivors' groups like Theos for spouses and Compassionate Friends for parents. Survivors often also attend single parent groups, singles groups, and special groups like Al-Anon.

Typically, the groups survivors attend are open-ended, meaning the participants change from meeting to meeting. Also, they usually do not follow goal-oriented formats. As helpful as support groups might be, they are not likely to meet the special needs of survivors early in bereavement, because they are not specifically structured to deal with the special grief reactions following suicide. The survivors often do not go back after only one or two meetings. Some survivors, continuing to search for a source of help, understanding, and encouragement, repeat this pattern in more than one support group.

Abandoning support groups is common among survivors in their first year of bereavement. Survivors waiting until after the second year, when grief has diminished and recovery is underway to some degree, benefit more from these same support groups. Support groups not directly focused upon the grief of suicide survivors seem to provide help in recovery but not in dealing with severe grief reactions. In other words, open-ended and general support groups do not adequately help the survivor resolve the many intense reactions and deeply painful experiences that are part and parcel of suicide survivorship.

Adina Wrobleski was involved in establishing grief support groups for suicide survivors early in the 1980s in Minneapolis, Minnesota. [81] Allen Battle studied groups in Memphis, Tennessee, during the same years. [82] Both recognized the difficulty suicide survivors encounter within support groups and recommended that they turn to groups that address unique features of suicide bereavement. Since the 1980s, suicide survivors' groups have been organized in many communities around the country.

Many suicide survivors' groups use an open structure in which membership is not fixed from one meeting to next, no agenda or predetermined topics are covered, and no limit is placed on the number of meetings. Size of these groups is usually not set, but rather is determined simply by the number of survivors who happen to attend any particular meeting. As few as five or six people might he present at one meeting and as many as fifteen to twenty at another.

Other survivors' groups follow grief-therapy formats in which the same survivors attend from start to completion, a structured format with specific goals is imposed upon the meetings, and a limit is established for the number of group meetings to be conducted. These groups usually include between six to twelve survivors.

The difference in formats is an important consideration. Individuals attending suicide survivors' groups can be anywhere between a few weeks to fifteen years or more beyond the suicide. Obviously, survivors in the early period of grief have different needs than those well past this stage, and one particular support group does not necessarily meet the needs of both.

How survivors respond to a grief support group largely depends on its structure and composition. Suicide survivors commonly find little satisfaction in open and non-structured suicide support groups when they are in the initial year of bereavement. They abandon these groups as frequently as they abandon the more general support groups mentioned above. Adina Wrobleski reported a 40% dropout rate among Suicide Survivor Support Groups in Minneapolis. The dropouts went to one or two meetings and did not return afterwards. The suicide survivors who give up on support groups likely are the individuals still in the most painful stages of grieving.

The needs of survivors early in their bereavement are best met in groups providing both structure and information focused upon the special features of suicide bereavement. Suicide grief-therapy groups more frequently follow this format than do open suicide support groups.

The primary goals of grief therapy are to facilitate the survivor's separation from the decedent and to promote healthy recovery from grief. To these ends, grief-therapy groups use structured formats dealing directly with grief experiences. Meetings are scheduled regularly over a period of several months to help survivors get through the trying stage of bereavement. Usually, ten to fifteen meetings, lasting 1.5 hours and held every two weeks, or a minimum of once monthly, are sufficient in meeting the therapeutic goals.

* * *

"Going to the meetings was like a safe haven. "

A Survivor

* * *

Regardless of structure and composition, effective suicide survivors' support groups focus on concerns related to the suicidal nature or the death. Issues and concerns especially important to suicide survivors include:

* Searching for the meaning of the death or for an explanation of the suicide.

* Dealing with mental images of the suicidal death.

* Dealing with negative social views and reactions toward suicide and the survivor—the stigma.

* Learning to talk about the death and decedent in an honest, non-defensive way.

* Resolving feelings of anger, depression, shame, blame, and guilt.

* Experiencing seemingly crazy, frightening, and confusing thoughts, feelings, or behaviors.

* Resolving doubts regarding the "normalcy" of bereavement.

* Exploring matters of faith and religion.

* Lifting the devastating loss of self-esteem.

* Breaking through the preoccupation with the suicidal nature of the death and getting on with bereavement.

* Repairing the survivor's life and family.

Suicide survivors unquestionably experience special benefits within suicide survivor groups, and grief-therapy groups have shown encouraging results. Allen Battle reported that most survivors participating in the Memphis "Survivor of Suicide" therapy groups believed their needs had been met in fewer than ten meetings. Remaining through ten to fifteen meetings helped some survivors. Only a few felt that being in a group had not helped. Bruce Danto reported that members of a suicide survivors group therapy program in the Detroit, Michigan area, quickly formed deep and meaningful relationships. [83]

Among other benefits suicide survivors commonly experience within these support groups are:

* Relief in sharing their stories with others able to identify compassionately with their grief.

* Increased understanding of the dynamics of suicide.

* Assistance in accepting the reality of the suicidal death.

* Support in working through the grief crisis and in dealing with stresses of daily living in the aftermath of the death.

* Opportunities to express feelings, including negative ones toward the deceased, in a supportive, non-threatening, and non-rejecting atmosphere.

* Encouragement to talk about, or hear about, the suicide over and over.

* Support and encouragement in helping children.

This last feature is a tremendous benefit for survivors participating in a suicide support group. As Lee Ann Hoff noted, parents may need special help in explaining a suicide to children. There is an almost universal wish to hide details of a suicide from children, usually arising from a mistaken belief that doing so spares them unnecessary pain.

Hoff maintained that parents often do not comprehend the serious results that are possible from trying to hide facts from children. She reminds us that children usually know more than they are given credit for and, in the least, know that something much more terrible than an accident has taken place. Hoff insisted that suicide is best explained clearly, simply, and in a manner consistent with a child's level of development and understanding. Encouraging children to ask questions and express feelings is also important.

Finding Suicide Survivors' Support Groups

This chapter has suggested that nearly three quarters of all survivors have grief concerns serious enough to try professional counseling at least once during their bereavement—but not early in the grief process when it would be most helpful for them to do so. This, and the fact that suicide survivors are difficult to identify through obituary articles, hampers postvention support efforts during the initial period of their grief.

At least a year passes after the death before many survivors look for professional help. In some cases, the motivation for doing so derives from the fact that, in a year's time, the effects of grieving accumulate. Surviving grief requires a reservoir of resilience, and any survivor can feel like she or he has exhausted all the personal resources available. In other cases, the survivor is simply unprepared for the duration of grief and becomes concerned something is wrong. In either case, a great number of survivors enlist the counseling support of some professional before the end of the second year. Additionally, many survivors attempt to ease the stresses of grieving by participating in a support group.

Since suicide survivors often initiate their own postvention efforts at some point, it is helpful for them to know where to look for assistance. Two community organizations can provide information about local survivor's support groups. Regional American Foundation for Suicide Prevention chapters have successfully modeled the wide use of media and advertising to alert suicide survivors to the availability of special services. Suicide Prevention and Crisis Centers are also appropriate places to inquire about the availability of services for survivors.

Several Internet sources provide updated listings of available suicide survivor groups in the United States. The American Association of Suicidology's *Directory of Survivors of Suicide Support Groups by State* (updated for this printing in September 2013), for example, provides a listing of 285 available support groups established in all fifty states and in the District of Columbia (see suicidology.org). The American Foundation for Suicide Prevention provides a more extensive directory listing 746 groups across the states (see afsp.org/coping-with-suicide/find-support/find-a-support-group).

* * *

"Come let me take your hand. For where
you must walk, I, too, have walked."

Paul Kinney, [84]

* * *

Attending a suicide survivors support group is recommended for all survivors, regardless of their relationship to the deceased—especially in their first year of their bereavement. Survivors can find comfort in having a chance to talk to and listen to others who have shared a similar experience in losing a loved one to self-inflicted death. Increased emotionality is natural for the survivors as feelings surface in their first few meetings, and some decide not to return to the group. However, the benefits of a support group typically increase by attending at least six meetings. Most survivors find that the initial discomfort of dealing with grief within a group decreases as familiarity with the group experience develops and connections are established with other members.

A useful rule of thumb is: "Attend six meetings, then decide if the group is helpful."

eleven
Further Conclusions

"A suicide is never completely forgotten or forgiven."
Pamela Cantor [85]

Patterns of Recovery

Suggestions that suicide survivors experience more frequent severe grief reactions have, in the past, led to the conclusion these survivors are inevitably doomed to complicated bereavement and troubled readjustments to life. This conclusion was simply not true. The belief that suicide shackles and torments its survivors more than other forms of death is largely a myth.

Although suicide bereavement often includes many special reactions, and its onslaught can nearly be overwhelming, outcome for survivors is more promising than might be expected. In fact, the outcome of suicide bereavement is similar to that of any other bereavement.

The majority of suicide survivors grieve and recover adequately and satisfactorily. These survivors eventually reestablish themselves in a life that holds meaning, purpose, satisfactions, and day-to-day concerns no longer directly tied to the experience grief. Of course, some suicide survivors do not fair well in grieving and recovery. For them, the suicide and its consequent grief are a devastating experience that impacts upon the rest of their lives. These survivors, victims of suicide, are in the unfortunate minority.

That the majority of adult survivors do well in the aftermath of suicide might be surprising, considering the grief they must negotiate. This does not imply that suicide survivors are not scarred by the death. They are. It is more accurate to say, however, that they and their lives are changed by the suicide, not destroyed by it.

Memories of the circumstances surrounding the suicide are likely to he imprinted vividly on the survivor's mind and remain so ten, fifteen, twenty years after the death. The suicidal event itself is unlikely to ever be forgotten. Many survivors continue to ask "why?" years after the suicide and never completely resolve the search for an explanation of the death. They also long regret the death on some level and fantasize how different life would be had it not happened.

Enduring reactions like these retain the emotional power to touch off sorrow. Yet, such lingering traces of grief do not tie suicide survivors endlessly to their bereavement. Like other survivors, most suicide survivors recover the capacity to find meaning, satisfaction, and enjoyment in life following their grief.

* * *

> "Only by living my grief fully will I be able to walk through it and learn what it has to tell me."
>
> Martha Whitmore Hickman. [86]

* * *

The ways by which suicide survivors accomplish their recoveries and re-adjustments are similar to those of other survivors. They often credit the resolution of grief to the availability of understanding friends or family, a deeply felt responsibility toward children still at home, a strong spiritual or religious faith, a life stable in all other aspects, a practical attitude toward death developed early in life (for example, "We all have to die sometime, and you have to make the most of things when you're left behind."), and/or just doing their best while giving grief free rein to run its course.

Talking through emotional grief reactions openly and honestly is crucial to successful bereavement. Denial or concealment of any aspect of the experience inhibits the grief process. It is particularly important that suicide survivors talk about the suicide and what it means to them. Survivors who recover satisfactorily are those able to confront the nature of the death and honestly deal with it.

Apparently, the opportunity to talk with anyone concerned enough to listen about the suicide and the grief reactions that follow it helps the survivor manage the grief. Whether suicide survivors talk with friends, family members, ministers, or professional counselors does not seem to matter. Among those who frequently talk about the death openly with others, satisfactory recovery and readjustment are the rule rather than the exception.

* * *

> "We talk now more about the life she loved and the values she showed us. Her suicide taught us not to take the lives of those we love for granted in any way or on any day."
>
> A Survivor

* * *

Survivors least likely to recover adequately from their grief seem to be those who either are isolated from understanding and supportive social contact or are unable to bring themselves to discuss the suicide. If a survivor does not talk honestly about the death, partially unfinished, repressed, or unresolved grief is a common result.

One universal consequence of inadequately completed grief is that future bereavement revitalizes buried grief, like reopening a festering wound. Survivors with unfinished grief suffer later emotional recollection of prior deaths whenever they experience new bereavements. Sometimes these survivors have to work through old grief in order to make sense of new grief.

It is not unusual for any survivor to re-experience an old grief during new bereavements, if in no other form than to have memories reemerge believed to have been long forgotten. Attendance at a funeral can trigger the images of an earlier funeral and another one before that going all the way back to childhood. Perhaps a hidden emotional thread unconsciously links all the grief events a person experiences in a lifetime.

How troublesome later resurrection of old grief becomes depends on how well grief associated to the suicide was resolved in the first place. If the earlier bereavement was curtailed or incomplete, a survivor will have to expend a great deal of energy either to complete the old grief or to keep it buried beneath psychological defenses weakened by current grief. Ultimately, the consequence of unfinished, repressed, or unresolved grief is that new bereavements can be all the more crippling when fueled by old grief.

The Intent To Die

To better understand a suicide survivor's grief experience, it is important to recognize that part of this experience is determined by social perceptions of self-inflicted death. As explained in Chapter Four, current cultural attitudes and conventions divide death into normal and suicidal, depending on the apparent cause of death.

It helps to recognize that the social belief that non-suicidal death is "normal" partially dictates the course that grief navigates. Following a suicide, grief is significantly influenced by the social belief that suicide is "not normal." As if swift, unexpected grief is not traumatic enough, suicide survivors suffer reactions resulting from the perceived inappropriateness of self-inflicted death.

Only after a suicide does the label attached to the death so intensely affect the survivor. Suicide survivors would not experience many of the additional grief reactions inherent only in self-inflicted death if suicidal death was accepted as a normal form of death rather than viewed as abnormal. The division of death into normal and suicidal (abnormal) potentially results in the special grief experiences described earlier, sometimes with devastating consequences for the suicide survivor. This result is unfortunate, because separation of death into normal and suicidal is based on false inferences by our society.

The common thread presumed to tie all deaths considered normal is the presumed absence of intention or wish to die on the part of the decedent. That deaths considered normal have this feature in common is a social illusion. Intent or wish to die in any death cannot be known with complete certainty. This is true in death by natural cause, accident, homicide, and suicide. There are suspected cases in which a person with a desire to die did so by means not obviously suicidal. Some people with terminal illness die before their prognosis would suggest they should. Patients who complete Living Wills are free to decline life-prolonging treatment. Many people die in car accidents that appear completely avoidable. Some homicide victims appear to have deliberately provoked fatal attacks.

Even though a person dies intentionally (whether by conscious or unconscious motive), if his intention is not obvious, the death will be labeled something other than suicide. Such deaths are considered normal and the survivor experiences a "normal" bereavement.

Deaths in which intent to die is absent but appears to be present are also common. Many deaths look like suicides, but are determined by investigations to have been accidents or homicides. Yet, if a death is an accident, but is labeled a suicide, the survivor experiences suicide bereavement, not accidental death bereavement.

Grief, therefore, is not entirely a reaction to the reality of the death itself: that is, the permanent loss of a loved one. It is also a reaction to the label given to the death by social convention.

It is impossible to know if the decedent intended to die, regardless of the *immediate cause and manner of death* documented on a death certificate. Once the post mortem label is applied, however, if the official cause of death is suicide, society draws the conclusion that the death was not "inevitable" at that time. This assumption is based on the belief that the decedent would have lived a much longer life had it not been for the suicide, without acknowledging any chance that the decedent's life could have ended just as abruptly by terminal illness, natural disaster, random homicide, or accident. On a deeper psychological level, this belief might serve as a defense against facing the realities of human death. More specifically, the strong reaction to this form of "premature" death might serve to unconsciously protect us from our own fear of dying.

We mortals have not learned to face and accept death. We are not comfortable with, nor do we like to acknowledge, the fact that death for any of us can be just an instant away. Part of our troubled reaction to suicide might be that it makes us confront death sooner than we feel necessary. Suicide disturbs us because it forces us to face issues surrounding death before such confrontation is "inevitable."

The Imprint Of Inevitability

Our society considers self-inflicted death to be an abnormal behavior, in part, because it brings death to the individual and grief to the survivors sooner than is acceptable. That a suicidal death did not have to happen is not the only feature that makes it "abnormal." If inevitability was the only factor, homicides and accidents, neither necessarily inevitable, might also be considered abnormal. This is not the case. Accidents and homicides are not viewed socially as abnormal. Suicide, on the other hand, arrives with a stigma attached. University students, intelligent adults, confirm that the death will not be accepted as normal or inevitable under any circumstances for more than 50% of the people who learn a death has been a suicide.

It is the combination of the intention to die and the apparent senseless nature of the death that leads us to view suicide as abnormal. Consequently, because suicidal death is perceived as neither "normal" nor as carrying the "imprint of inevitability," an absolute mandate for its prevention has been generated. Is there any other form of death with such a weighty mandate?

Preventing Suicide

The demand to prevent suicide has social, legal, and moral roots. When a suicide occurs, the mandate for its prevention weighs heavily upon the survivors with powerful social, legal, and moral implications. The survivors bear the brunt when the mandate for preventing suicide fails.

Society seems psychologically and emotionally blind to the fact that preventing suicide is a difficult endeavor at best, but also is, in important ways, an act that forestalls eventual death. Must we prolong life regardless of the consequences or the quality of the life preserved for the individual?

Professionals working in the field of suicide prevention react strongly to questions of this nature. Rightly so. Preventing someone's death is a compassionate and humane endeavor. Life-saving efforts are especially humane when the quality of the person's life is somehow enhanced and improved after the prevention.

A person's life is not always made better by its saving. In some cases, preventing a person from ending his or her life is nothing short of a sentence to live out a hopeless, painful, and humiliating life; a life devoid of anything that might be considered humanly satisfying. The compassion and humanity in interfering with an individual's choice of putting an end to such pain, regardless of how distasteful this alternative is to us, is a sensitive topic and open to debate. It is the same debate that often erupts in families when a patient's Living Will dictates that no life-saving measures are to be taken by medical personnel.

Thomas S. Szasz was an American psychiatrist who often challenged and debated the right and wrong of mental illness treatment. At the time, his opinions were considered controversial. Szasz insisted that suicide was a basic human right and that the State was not to regulate the responsibility for others to prevent individuals from taking their own lives or to allow coercive interventions. [87]

In America over the last twenty-five years, the Supreme Court has reviewed state court decisions involving whether or not the right to die is a liberty protected by the Constitution's *Due Process Clause* and allowed to individuals with a terminal illness or in great pain. In July and September 1989, the Michigan and Georgia courts ruled in favor of allowing paralyzed adults to make their own right-to-die decisions. [88] In 1990, the issue of whether a 33-year-old woman's feeding tube could be disconnected by her family was argued in Missouri. Other right-to-die cases were debated in Washington State in 1997 and in Oregon in 2006. A Montana court ruled in 2009 that the right to die applies to those with life-threatening medical conditions, and a law went into effect in Vermont on May 20, 2013, permitting physicians to prescribe a lethal dose of medication to patients with a terminal illness.

At this point in time, it is legal only in Washington, Oregon, Montana, and Vermont for a physician or other third party to give a patient the lethal means to end his or her own life: That is, to assist in "self-intentioned cessation of life."

Suicide: a Normal Death?

Our society is hesitant, perhaps frightened, to accept the premise that, if death is normal, so too must be death by suicide. Perhaps we are afraid that accepting suicide as a normal death might somehow be an endorsement of suicidal acts. This need not be the case.

This is not a matter of advocating or even condoning suicide. We will never *like* self-inflicted death, regardless of the circumstances of the decedent's life. The question posed here is, can we stop viewing suicide as a sin, a weakness of character, an act of insanity, an extreme expression of inherent selfishness, a symptom of family discord, or as a failure of others to respond in a caring and timely way? Can we instead accept suicide as a normal means of death? Can we accept suicide as a normal reaction to chronic and severe depression, a normal behavioral response to a yet undiscovered neuro-chemical disturbance or biological imbalance, a normal consequence of a life sadly rife with incomprehensible pain, suffering, and hopelessness, or as an unfortunate, but normal, consequence of an ill-considered impulse that temporarily steals away a person's ability to think and behave rationally? Difficult questions, yes.

The objective of this book is not to argue the right or wrong of self-inflicted death. The hope expressed here is that suicide survivors will be freed from the adverse grief reactions engendered by society's views of death by suicide. Obviously, our social views have had little success in preventing suicide. Nor do our conventions have any impact upon the decedent once the act has been completed.

Our social views and attitudes do, however, carry serious implications and consequences for the suicide survivor, the innocent victim of self-inflicted death. Acceptance of suicide as a "normal" form of death will remove the stigma and might well diminish the special experiences of suicide survivors.

Suicide survivors are likely to continue grieving in the manner described in this book. They are likely to continue to do so for as long as social illusions stigmatize suicidal death as somehow very different than other forms of death. Yet, suicide survivors' bereavements are normal, dictated in part by a significant personal loss, by an unexpected and other-than-natural death, and, finally, by a death socially viewed as abnormal.

Grief reactions resulting from the significant loss and from the unexpected and other-than-natural features of suicide are not likely to change. However, suicide survivors need not be damned to experience such unique grief reactions like denial of the cause of death, embarrassment regarding the death, fear of insanity, moral concerns, or communication problems. Social beliefs and attitudes can change. Myths can be assailed. If such changes are fostered regarding the experience of suicide in our society, the grief experience of its survivors will hopefully be relieved of the additional reactions resulting from the socially-viewed inappropriateness of the death.

The Survivors' Entitlement

The challenge presented is that we all, survivors, family members, friends, and professional helpers alike, strive tirelessly and diligently to provide suicide survivors the dignity to which the experience of bereavement entitles them.

NOTES

1. Karl A. Menninger. Foreword, in E. Shneidman & N. Farberow (Eds.), *Clues to Suicide*, New York: McGraw-Hill Book Company, 1957.

2. R. Hirschfeld & L. Davidson. Risk factors for suicide, in Allen J. Frances & Robert E. Hales (Eds.), *Review of Psychiatry, Volume 7*, Washington, D.C.: American Psychiatric Press, 1988, pp. 307–33.

3. Ronald W. Maris. *Pathways to Suicide*, Baltimore: John Hopkins University Press, 1981, p. 30.
4. Bob Herbert. The Lunatic's Manual, Tuesday, *New York Times*, August 3, 2010, and Editorial: When Warriors Hurt Themselves, Thursday, *New York Times*, September 1, 2010, Page A34.
5. Understanding Suicide and its Impact, PSYC 381/793, was developed at the North Dakota State University Psychology Department.

6. M. C. Kearl and R. Harris. Individualism & the emerging "modern" ideology of death, *Omega*, <u>12</u>, 1981, pp. 269–80.

7. G. P. Ginsburg. Public conceptions and attitudes about suicide, *Journal of Health & Social Behavior,* <u>12</u>, 1971, pp. 200–207.

8. Edwin S. Shneidman. Introduction. In E. Shneidman (Ed.), *Suicidology: Contemporary Developments*, New York: Grune & Stratton, 1976.

9. Edwin S. Shneidman. *Deaths of Man,* New York: Quadrangle Books, 1973.

10. A. L. Berman. Research Note: Estimating the population of survivors of suicide: Seeking an evidence base, *Suicide and Life-Threatening Behavior*, 41(1), 2011, pp. 110–16.

11. Louis Wekstein. *Handbook of Suicidology: Principles, problems, and practice*, New York: Bruner/Mazel, 1979.

12. Alfred Alvarez. *The Savage God: Study of Suicide*, New York: Random House, 1972, p. 91.

13. Suzanne Gerber. Next Avenue: What Does The Exploding Rate Of Boomer Suicide Say About Us?, *Forbes* Magazine, June 7, 2013.

14. Arnold Toynbee. The relationship between life & death, living & dying, in E. Shneidman (Ed.), *Death: Current Perspectives*, Palo Alto: Mayfield, 1976, pp. 324–32.

15. *Much Ado About Nothing*, Act III, Scene II, Benedick speaks.

16. Edwin S. Shneidman. Postvention: The care of the bereaved, *Suicide & Life-Threatening Behavior*, 11, 1981, pp. 349–59.

17. Colin Parkes and Robert Weiss. *Recovery from Bereavement*, New York: Basic Books, Inc, 1983.

18. Erich Lindemann. Acute grief: Symptoms & Management, *American Journal of Psychiatry*, 101, 1944, pp. 141–48.

19. John Bowlby. Process of Mourning, *International Journal of Psychoanalysis*, 42, 1961, pp. 317–40.

20. Colin Parkes. *Bereavement Studies of Grief in Adult Life*, New York: International University Press, 1972.

21. Edwin S. Shneidman. Foreword, in A. Cain (Ed.), *Survivors of Suicide*, Springfield, IL: C. C. Thomas, 1972.

22. Edwin S. Shneidman. To the bereaved of a suicide, in B. Danto & A. Kutscher (Eds.), *Suicide & Bereavement*, New York: Arno Press, 1977, pp. 67–69.

23. Colin Parkes and Robert Weiss. *Recovery from Bereavement*, New York: Basic Books, Inc, 1983.

24. Wayne Weiten. *Psychology: Themes and variations*, Pacific Grove, CA: Brooks/Cole, 1989, p. 547.

25. Samuel E. Wallace. Three ways of dying, in S. Wallace (Ed.), *After Suicide*, New York: John Wiley & Sons, 1973, p.118.

26. Reprinted from the American Association of Suicidology *Surviving Suicide Newsletter*, Winter 1993.

27. Atlanta, Georgia: Chalice Press, 2005.

28. John Hewett. *After Suicide*, Philadelphia: Westminster Press, 1980, pp. 34–51.

29. Edwin S. Shneidman. Introduction, in E. Shneidman (Ed.), *Suicidology: Contemporary Developments*, New York: Grune & Stratton, 1976.

30. Samuel E. Wallace. The cost of suicide. In S. Wallace (Ed.), *After Suicide*, New York: John Wiley & Sons, 1973, p. 229.

31. Alfred Alvarez. *The Savage God: Study of Suicide*, New York: Random House, 1972, p. 107.

32. Ronald W. Maris. *Pathways to Suicide*, Baltimore: John Hopkins University Press, 1981, p. 336.

33. Edwin S. Shneidman. Introduction, in E. Shneidman (Ed.), *Suicidology: Contemporary Developments*, New York: Grune & Stratton, 1976.

34. G. P. Ginsburg. Public conceptions and attitudes about suicide, *Journal of Health & Social Behavior*, 12, 1971, pp. 200–207.

35. Samuel E. Wallace. Three ways of dying, in S. Wallace (Ed.), *After Suicide*. New York: John Wiley & Sons, 1973, pp. 107, 203, 205.

36. Rick Elder. A Sibling Viewpoint, reprinted from *Suicide Bereavement Support Newsletter*, Volume 14, Number 10, October 2002, South Bay, California.

37. Erich Lindemann. Acute grief: Symptoms & Management, *American Journal of Psychiatry*, 101, 1944, pp. 141–48.

38. Lyla Jackson. Reprinted from the American Association of Suicidology *Surviving Suicide Newsletter*, Summer/Fall 1997.

39. Sue Chance. *Stronger than Death: When Suicide Touches Your Life*, New York: W.W. Norton & Company, 1992, p. 50.

40. Erich Lindemann & Ina M. Greer. A study of grief emotional responses to suicide, *Pastoral Psychology*, 4, 1953, pp. 9–13.

41. T. H. Holmes & R. H. Rahe. The Social Readjustment Rating Scale, *Journal of Psychosomatic Research*, 11(2), 1967, pp. 213–18.

42. Colin Parkes. The broken heart, in E. Shneidman (Ed.), *Death: Current Perspectives*, Palo Alto: Mayfield, 1976, pp. 333–46.

43. Kjell Erik Rudestam. Physical & psychological responses to suicide in the family, *Journal of Consulting & Clinical Psychology*, 45, 1977, pp. 162–70.

44. Colin Parkes and Robert Weiss. *Recovery from Bereavement*, New York: Basic Books, Inc, 1983.

45. Edwin S. Shneidman. Prevention, intervention, & postvention, *Annals of Internal Medicine*, 75, 1971, pp. 453–458, and Fifty-Eight Years in E. Shneidman & N. Farberow (Eds.), *Clues to Suicide*, New York: McGraw-Hill Book Company, 1957, p. 22.

46. Karl A. Menninger. *Man against himself*, New York: Halcourt Brace Jovanovich, 1938, p. 35.

47. William Steele. *Preventing teenage suicide: The second leading cause of death among the nation's youth*, Naples, FL: Ann Arbor Publishers, 1983.

48. Karl A. Menninger. *Man against himself*, New York: Halcourt Brace Jovanovich, 1938, p. 71.

49. Ronald W. Maris. *Pathways to Suicide*, Baltimore: John Hopkins University Press, 1981, p. 69.

50. John Hewett. *After Suicide*, Philadelphia: Westminster Press, 1980, pp. 28–30.

51. Suniya S. Luthar, Dante Cicchetti, and Bronwyn Becker. The construct of resilience: A critical evaluation and guidelines for future work, *Child Development*, 71, 2000, pp. 543–562.

52. Alfred Alvarez. *The Savage God: Study of Suicide*, New York: Random House, 1972, p. 259.

53. Karl A. Menninger. *Man against himself,* New York: Halcourt Brace Jovanovich, 1938, p. 22.

54. Herbert Hendin. *Suicide in America, 2nd Edition,* New York: W. W. Norton & Company, 1995.

55. Kay Redfield Jamison. *Night Falls Fast: Understanding Suicide,* New York: Alfred A. Knopf, 1999.

56. George Howe Colt. *November of the Soul: The Enigma of Suicide,* New York: Scribner, 2006.

57. Edwin S. Shneidman. Prevention, intervention, & postvention, *Annals of Internal Medicine,* 75, 1971, pp. 453–58.

58. M. Goldberg & E. Mudd. The effects of suicidal behavior upon marriage and the family, in L. P. Resnik (Ed.), *Suicidal Behavior: Diagnosis and Management,* Boston: Little, Brown, and Company, 1968, pp. 348–56.

59. Ronald W. Maris. *Pathways to Suicide,* Baltimore: John Hopkins University Press, 1981, p. 267.

60. Edward Dunne & Karen Dunne-Maxim. Preface, in E. Dunne, J. McIntosh, & K. Dunne-Maxim (Eds.), *Suicide and its aftermath: Understanding and counseling the survivors,* New York: W. W. Norton & Company, 1987, p. xvi.

61. Morris E. Chafetz and H. W. Demone. *Alcoholism and Society,* New York: Oxford University Press, 1962, p. 14.

62. Sarah Waters. *The Little Stranger,* New York: Riverhead Books, 2009, p. 445.

63. Mark Solomon. The bereaved & stigma of suicide, *Omega*, 13, 1982, p. 377–87.

64. *Collected Poems of Edna St. Vincent Millay*, New York: Harper & Row Publishers, 1981, p. 562.

65. Charles Neuringer. Bereavement reactions in survivors of suicide, in B. Dante & A. Kutscher (Eds.), *Suicide & Bereavement*, New York: Arno Press, 1977, p. 150–62.

66. Karl A. Menninger. *Man against himself*, New York: Halcourt Brace Jovanovich, 1938, p. 44.

67. Robert Kastenbaum. Suicide as a preferred way of death, in E.Shneidman (Ed.), Suicidology: Contemporary Developments, New York: Grune & Stratton, 1976, pp. 421–41.

68. Pamela Cantor. The effects of youthful suicide on the family, *Psychiatric Opinion*, 12, 1975, pp. 6–11.

69. Victor E. Frankl. *Man's Search for Meaning*, Boston: Beacon Press, 1959, p. 6.

70. John McIntosh. Survivor family relationships: Literature review, in E. Dunne, J. McIntosh, & K. Dunne-Maxim (Eds.), *Suicide and its aftermath: Understanding and counseling the survivors*, New York: W. W. Norton & Company, 1987, pp. 73–84.

71. Erich Lindemann. Acute grief: Symptoms & Management, *American Journal of Psychiatry*, 101, 1944, pp. 141–48.

72. Kjell Erik Rudestam. Physical & psychological responses to suicide in the family, *Journal of Consulting & Clinical Psychology*, 45, 1977, pp. 162–70.

73. Recollection of Jim Bailey, 87, as reported by Brian Albrecht, in Servicemen forever changed by brutality on Okinawa, *Cleveland Plain Dealer*, Saturday, March 30, 2013, Page B1.

74. Lionel Lawson, Sergeant, USMC Retired, in correspondence, Saturday, August 17, 2013.

75. William Coleman. *Understanding Suicide*, Elgin, IL: David C. Cook Publishing Company, 1979.

76. Edwin S. Shneidman. *Deaths of Man*, New York: Quadrangle Books, 1973.

77. Edwin S. Shneidman. Postvention: The care of the bereaved, *Suicide & Life-Threatening Behavior*, 11, 1981, pp. 349–59.

78. Lee Ann Hoff. Helping survivors of suicide, in *People in Crisis: Understanding & Helping*, Boston, MA: Addison-Wesley Publishing, 1978, pp. 142–47.

79. Donna Junghardt. A program in postvention, in Corrine Hatton, Sharon Valente, & Alice Rink (Eds.), *Suicide: Assessment & Intervention*, New York: Appleton, Century, Crofts, 1977, pp. 124–32.

80. The American Foundation for Suicide Prevention. See Web site at afsp.org.

81. Adina Wrobleski. The suicide survivors grief group, *Omega*, 15, 1984, p. 173–84.

82. Allen O. Battle. Group therapy for survivors of suicide, *The Journal of Crisis Intervention and Suicide Prevention*, Volume 5(1), July 1984, pp. 45–58.

83. Bruce Danto. Project SOS: Volunteers in action with survivors of suicide, in B. Dante & Austin H. Kutscher (Eds.), *Suicide & Bereavement*, New York: Arno Press, 1977, pp. 222–39.

84. Paul Kinney. Louisville, Kentucky, from *The Compassionate Friends Newsletter*, April 1999.

85. Pamela Cantor. The effects of youthful suicide on the family, *Psychiatric Opinion*, 12, 1975, pp. 6–11.

86. Martha Whitmore Hickman. *Healing After Loss: Daily Meditations For Working Through Grief*, New York: Avon Books, Inc, 1994, p. 27.

87. Thomas Stephen Szasz. The Ethics of Suicide, in his *The Theology of Medicine*: The Political-Philosophical Foundation of Medical Ethics, New York: Harper Colophon, 1971, pp. 68–85.

88. Ethics: Death Wish, *Time* Magazine, Monday, September 18, 1989, p. 67. A 33-year-old Georgia quadriplegic won the rights to turn off the ventilator that had been keeping him alive for four years and to end his life.

SELECTED RESOURCES

American Association of Suicidology, 202-237-2280, www.suicidology.org (Click on "Suicide loss survivors").

American Foundation for Suicide Prevention, 888-333-2377 (toll-free), www.afsp.org (Click on "Surviving Suicide Loss").

Victoria G. Alexander. *Words I Never Thought to Speak: Stories of Life in the Wake of Suicide.* New York: Lexington Books, 1991.

Bob Baugher and Jack Jordan. *After Suicide Loss: Coping With Your Grief.* Available through the American Foundation for Suicide Prevention Web site, 2002.

Iris Bolton and Curtis Mitchell. *My Son... My Son: A Guide to Healing After Death, Loss, or Suicide.* Atlanta, Georgia: The Bolton Press, 1995.

Beverly Cobain and Jean Larch. *Dying to Be Free: A Health Guide for Families after a Suicide.* Center City, Minneapolis: Hazelden Foundation, 2006.

George Howe Colt. *November of the Soul: The Enigma of Suicide.* New York: Scribner, 2006.

Arrington Cox and Ruthanne (Candy) Neely Arrington. *Aftershock: Help, Hope, and Healing in the Wake of Suicide.* Nashville, Tennessee: B & H Publishing, 2003.

Carla Fine. *No Time to Say Goodbye: Surviving The Suicide Of A Loved One.* Main Street Books, 1997.

Herbert Hendin. *Suicide in America.* New York: W. W. Norton & Company, 1995

John H. Hewett. *After Suicide.* Philadelphia, PA: Westminster Press, 1980.

Albert Y. Hsu. *Grieving a Suicide: A Loved One's Search for Comfort, Answers & Hope.* Downers Grove, Illinois: InterVarsityPress, 2002.

Kay Redfield Jamison. *Night Falls Fast: Understanding Suicide.* New York: Alfred A. Knopf, 1999.

Christopher Lukas and Henry Seiden. *Silent Grief: Living in the Wake of Suicide.* Philadelphia, PA: Jessica Kingsley Publishers, 2007.

Anne McCracken and Mary Semel (Eds.). *A Broken Heart Still Beats: After Your Child Dies.* Center City, Minneapolis: Hazelden Publishing & Educational Services, 1998.

Alan D. Wolfelt. *Understanding Your Suicide Grief: Ten Essential Touchstones for Finding Hope and Healing Your Heart,* Fort Collins, Colorado: Companion Press, 2009.

ABOUT THE AUTHOR

TERENCE W. BARRETT graduated from the College of Wooster, Ohio. He served seven years in the U.S. Marine Corps. He earned advanced degrees from the University of Southern California, North Dakota State University, and the University of North Dakota. He retired from the North Dakota Air National Guard after twenty years of military service. A licensed psychologist, he practices in Fargo, ND, travels across the states to present seminars, and teaches at North Dakota State University. He was the charter president of the ND Chapter of the American Foundation for Suicide Prevention and is a clinical consultant at the Fargo VET Center.

CPSIA information can be obtained
at www.ICGtesting.com
Printed in the USA
LVHW051749300719
625873LV00011B/858